The Middle Generation

The Middle Generation

by Dr. Rose N. Franzblau

HOLT, RINEHART AND WINSTON
New York　　　*Chicago*　　　*San Francisco*

24578

To My Beloved Husband

CONTENTS

PREFACE

The Middle Generation is the one most often "lost in the crowd," standing between the younger "Rebel" Generation, and the older "Senior Citizen" Generation, both of which are continuously in the spotlight. It is nevertheless the keystone in the arch of our society and probably contributes the most to the welfare and stability of our nation.

The Middle Generation can be defined as the group whose parents are still alive, and who have children of their own. The youngest of them are newlyweds of one or two years' standing who have a newborn infant, and the oldest are people who may have grandchildren of their own, but whose parents are still living.

Numerically, they are in the minority. The youth (those under twenty-one) are increasing in numbers and in their proportion of the total population (about forty percent). The older group (those sixty-five and over, constituting ten percent), are benefiting from the advanced medical discoveries of the last half-century and the improvement in medical care and social security, and are living longer and staying healthier than ever before. The Middle Generation, roughly those between twenty-five and fifty-five, now comprises about twenty-five percent of the population, and by 1990, when the census is estimated to reach three hundred million, will include about twenty percent.

They are betwixt and between, having to contend with not one, but two generation gaps, between them and their children, and between them and their parents.

The problems they must face and handle include, on one side, those of their children, the new, turned-on, sexually "liberated," rebellious youth, who have progressed from draft-card burning to bank burning. On the other side, they must care for parents who can no longer care for themselves, still active parents who reserve the right to direct and criticize them just as when they were little, and a wide variety of other parents who present their own unique problems and dilemmas. Their own Middle Generation problems, by no means inconsiderable, are sandwiched in between.

These Middle Generation problems are unique unto themselves. There are jealousies, role reversals, interference with the child-rearing of the youngest generation, and alignments between the grandparents and grandchildren against the parents. There are special problems that arise when the grandparents have to live in the same house as the parents and children, three generations, sometimes six decades apart, all under the same roof.

In addition, when the children are in college or married, and the Middle Generation parents are alone again, they have new sex problems, stemming from the menopausal situation, or the new look at the spouse, which freedom from the former burdens of family care makes possible. Even when the marriage course is all set and the sailing is smooth and happy, the back-to-work and back-to-school impulses may lead to complications. We must also remember the rising mortality rates which come with increasing age. Death, ever a stranger, comes to visit the Middle Generation more often than in the younger years, and also strikes harder. When it does, the Middle Generation survivor finds carrying on much more difficult. Age, loss of flexibility, decline of physical energies and virility, and economic problems often make finding a new life-partner and adjusting to a new life-situation much more difficult.

These and many other problems, some of them characteristic of our own times alone, trouble the Middle Generation today. In the past the emphasis was upon the similarities and the closeness between them and the other two generations. Today it is more upon differences and points of conflict, although the three generations can and often still do live peacefully together in the same family unit.

This book focuses on the Middle Generation, which speaks for itself in these pages, in its own words, presenting concerns and problems of broad range and universal interest, and asking for clarification, guidance and help.

Nevertheless, this book really addresses itself to all three generations which are so closely related and involved with each other.

Many of the letters which I answer in my daily newspaper column and radio program come, not only from the Middle Generation, but from their children or parents, who have to cope with the problems which may be created from either side of the relationship. Thus, the book presents a cross section, culled from real-life situations, of human relations in our times.

Hopefully, all generations will find some helpful insights and suggestions for coping with the problems of inter-generation inter-relations, and some guidelines for correcting their own troubled or troublesome behavior, which sometimes is the cause of their own unhappiness, as well as that of others.

I wish to express my thanks to all at the New York *Post* and in the WCBS organization who have helped in my work from which the material presented in this book was drawn.

I wish also to express warm appreciation to Sol Stember and Mrs. Cecile Miller for their unfailing help in the research and editorial work which preparation of this book required.

New York, N.Y   ROSE N. FRANZBLAU, Ph.D.
June, 1970

The Middle Generation

PART I

Middle Generation Parents and Their Children

✺ 1. SEX AND THE CHILDREN OF THE MIDDLE GENERATION

Of all the problems that face the Middle Generation, those of a sexual nature are likely to be most upsetting. This is because the personal attitudes and values they involve stem from a highly private and sensitive area.

Parental sexual attitudes and conflicts are inevitably reflected in their children's sexual attitudes and behavior, and the manner in which they as parents deal with them.

The so-called "sexual revolution" now in progress makes things much harder for today's Middle Generation parents, especially those with teenagers who are caught up in the new sex morality.

When parents in their middle years are still enjoying very active sex lives of their own, they feel guilty about any restrictions they may wish to impose on the sex lives of their budding youngsters. This often makes them over-permissive or overly restrictive, and if they discover any acting-out on the part of their teenagers, they may become over-punitive and under-understanding. In every case, it makes them embarrassed to talk about sex with their teenagers, when they ask for instruction and guidance. The children get the feeling, sometimes, that their roles should be reversed—they could teach their parents.

Despite the widespread freeing of sexual inhibitions and easing of taboos, and with all the frankness and direct channels of communication which now exist between parents and children, many members of the Middle Generation cling to certain misconceptions. In fact, it is becoming increasingly clear that frankness, openness and even license do not necessarily lead to greater knowledge about sex, or deeper insight into sexual problems.

Children's sexual awareness and their sex drives keep pace with their physical and mental growth. This inevitably affects the parents' sex lives. They are challenged by their off-springs' youth and vigor, and are sometimes competitive with them sexually. It also leads to a recrudescence of the old opposite-sex-parent crushes and desires, if any residuals of the childhood wish remain unresolved. After all, it is not a baby anymore that the parent is dealing with, but an attractive, blossoming young adult. The tables have turned, and the drive is parent-for-child, rather than the other way around.

Middle Generation parents need a clear definition of the role they should play in guiding their children's sexual development, and a clear concept of the ethical and moral value system they believe in and would like to pass on to their children. It would also be helpful if they could be apprised of the sort of warning signals that children send out when there is danger ahead.

I

It is quite unanimously agreed that when a parent acts as a teacher in the sexual education of a child, strict gender lines should be followed. Fathers should teach sons and mothers should teach daughters. Any cross-over is usually unwise and can lead to unwanted and unfortunate results.

The motives of a parent who insists on providing the sex education of a child of the opposite sex, and who defends the practice, are suspect and should be closely examined. The likelihood is that it is done for the benefit of the parent, and not for that of the child. This is a case in point.

LETTER: *A conflict between my husband and myself is putting severe strains on my marriage. It concerns the raising of my thirteen-year-old son.*

My husband objects to my habit of permitting my son to take showers with me.

As one who was brought up in a liberal atmosphere, I am convinced that such attitudes in this area are the wisest. I have argued that it is better that my son learn early from me, than later—or too late—from the gutter. I allow my son a certain leeway when we are together and encourage him to ask questions.

How am I "corrupting" my son? That he does not have any guilt or shame about anything is proved by the fact that we have been able to discuss freely the most intimate normal bodily processes and functions.

I am in my late thirties. My husband is forty-three. We remarried three years ago. I was a widow, he a divorcé with no children.

ANSWER: Your husband feels that the exposure and practices to which you are subjecting your son might make for emotional retardation and instability. And he is right.

The harm done your son is aggravated by the fact that, deep down, you are fully aware that the arguments you present to justify this mutual exhibitionism and indulgence are only rationalizations.

Years ago, when the subject of sex became free for discussion, some people and parents went overboard. Total permissiveness prevailed in the name of progressiveness. But it was soon seen as a block, rather than an incentive to healthy psycho-sexual development.

Children become aware of sex, even if on a childish level, at the age of three or so. The questions that arise then revolve about the sexual activities of the parents. But at your son's age, sex becomes a very personal thing, and revolves around himself.

Unfortunately, the method you have pursued serves only to excite the child and arouse desires which both frighten and overwhelm him. He is afraid to move forward, for fear that should his wishes and excitations show, he would be punished and hurt most severely.

When you lost a husband, and the boy a father, you may have used your son unconsciously as the male in your life, giving him these extra privileges in the name of pro-gressivism.

With the arrival of your present husband, there also came the feeling that you had left him for another man. Through the exhibitionism, which was continued, you told him, without words, that he is still an intimate part of your life.

Before your son begins to show untoward results, you ought to get some counseling from a qualified expert in the field of child psychology. You need it for a clarification of the motives which make you pit a grown man and a growing boy against each other for your love, and the boy needs it to avert what might happen to his sexual development as a result of this practice. In the meantime, you ought to stop this practice at once.

II

Even in this day and age, one occasionally finds parents in the Middle Generation whose knowledge of sex is so limited that they manage to pass on not information, but ignorance, to their children. Such a parent may suddenly "discover" her child's unpreparedness, only when that child is on the verge of marriage.

The problem goes a little deeper than concern over the child's lack of sexual knowledge, but very likely relates to the parent's own sex attitudes and conflicts, as in this unusual case.

LETTER: *I have a nineteen-year-old daughter, a freshman in college, who is engaged and will be married in the summer. But I have found out that she knows very little about sex.*

How can I tell her what will be expected of her? Are there any good books on this subject?

I was married at twenty-one, but was as green as my daughter is now. She is thinking in terms of continuing her education. The boy is twenty-two and will graduate from college in June. They have nothing. His parents are for this marriage, but my husband and I are doubtful. We want our daughter to be happy.

ANSWER: Knowledge of the facts is not in and of itself an adequate preparation for sex in marriage.

A girl who falls in love with a man and plans her marriage with a sense of timeliness and rightness, may be assumed to have arrived at a fairly mature state of sexual readiness and awareness. All young couples become a little apprehensive about sex in their marriages, in the beginning. They wonder whether they will be adequate and satisfying to their mates, whether they will pass the test of bringing pleasure to the other and finding pleasure themselves.

As they near this high point in their lives, some of the old taboos and fears left over from childhood, and until now quiescent, begin to rumble again. The boy may be anxious about whether he will be potent enough. A girl with a latent fear of the sex act, especially of masculine aggressiveness, wonders whether it will immobilize her or whether it will be overcome by her desire for her husband.

Helpful guidance about such problems can best be given, first, by a gynecologist, and then, if need be, by a psychiatrist or a marriage counselor. A parent is about the last person who should attempt it, or who could do this job well, for there is too much emotional involvement between them all. The parent would tend to spotlight her own fears and failures, rather than her successes and satisfactions. She might be ashamed to discuss the latter with her child. If she is young enough still to be engaging vigorously in sex, sex education may seem to her an exhibitionistic way of telling about her own sex life. Her tendency would then be to avoid the subject.

The puzzlement is how you could have waited this long to inform your daughter about sex, especially after going into your own marriage so green and unknowledgeable.

The chances are that your daughter knows more about sex than you think. Similarly, when you married, you probably knew more about the subject than you cared, either then or now, to admit.

When you say that these two young people have nothing, you are evidently referring only to material things. Being in love with each other and willing to work and build together, there is every promise that they will have a good and fulfilling life. As a college graduate, your daughter's fiancé must have some area in which he is prepared vocationally. He should not have any difficulty in getting a job.

While the young couple hope to be able to get along on what he makes, it will not spoil them if the parents continue to pay at least her school expenses and, if possible, the balance which you would pay if she were still living at home. Any help that you can give would be an encouragement to her to finish college. It would also be a solid testimonial to your faith in her promise to you (as well as to herself) that she will complete her education.

You may feel very green, or perhaps too young, to be the mother of a marriageable daughter. If you are hesitant about discussing her future sex life with her you should suggest where they can go for this information. With their marriage still six months off, there is plenty of time to muster your courage and discuss the subject with her.

III

Loosening the ties that bind mothers and sons can be difficult and sometimes painful. However, by the time a son enters young manhood, the emotional separation should have been accomplished. If something has retarded the process, it usually carries deep-seated sexual overtones and connotations. These must be corrected lest the young man be deflected from the path of normal development.

The mother and son relationship below is a striking example of this process, and is a mirror-image of the usual behavior.

LETTER: *We have been married twenty-five years, and have two children. We have had our spats during these years, but they were not insurmountable. In the past year, however, we haven't gotten along well at all.*

All this is only incidental to the real problem. Our younger child, a boy, nineteen, attends college. He was a normal boy, though never an extrovert. He liked playing ball with his friends, and on occasion would go out with them. Now, however, he never goes with his friends. He is drawing closer to his mother, and she encourages him. When he is in the bathroom, she finds reasons to go in there. Also, when she takes a bath or attends to personal needs, he remembers something that he wanted to ask her, and without knocking, just walks in.

What should I do to bring our life back to normal?

ANSWER: Mothers find it as difficult to let go of their sons, as fathers do of their daughters. This mutual attachment of parent and child of opposite sex begins very early in childhood, and is quite universal. It becomes a problem only when the parent encourages the relationship too strongly and does not permit the child to become free of this dependency.

Thus, in adolescence, a son with too strong an attachment to his mother will make her his confidante in all his affairs of the heart, and go to her, rather than to his father, for information on sex matters. He does not need to have too close a relationship with girls or to go out too much, for he finds enough of the satisfactions he seeks in his close verbal relationship with his mother.

That is why the sons of such mothers sometimes stay unmarried altogether, or postpone marriage as long as their mothers are alive. To establish a lasting relationship with a woman seems to them to be an act of infidelity to the first woman in their lives, their mother. Sometimes, such men will enter into a secret relationship with a woman, or have close relationships with men. These do not evoke this same feeling of being treacherous or disloyal to their mothers.

Your wife ought to be made aware of the bad effects which this new "open-door policy" may have on her son. Such peeping and prying into each other's privacy represents, in a very real sense, a form of sexual stimulation. She must draw the line at this kind of mutual intrusion which attempts to restore the little-boy big-mother relationship of long ago. To permit this behavior to be resumed now can make your son's problem a really serious one.

Your son's emotional life should be his own private affair. Made aware through psychological counseling of the harmful effects of her behavior, your wife will surely put an end to it. It might give your son the strength to move away and build a life of his own. If this does not happen within a reasonable time, your son should start treatment on his own before he withdraws any further.

IV

Next to homosexuality, promiscuity is probably the hardest sexual problem for parents to face, particularly if the promiscuous child is a girl. Aside from the danger of pregnancy or venereal infection, the social penalties suffered by promiscuous women are far greater than those suffered by promiscuous men.

The motivations, conscious and unconscious, that account for such behavior patterns may be deeply rooted in the parent-child relationship. Somewhere under the surface lie certain basic unsatisfied needs of childhood. Somewhere under the callous façade of the promiscuous child like the one described below, is a suffering soul calling for help.

LETTER: *We have been married over twenty-five years. We have two daughters, one married and one in college.*

About a year ago, we learned that our younger daughter has had sexual relations with several young men. After a scene, she finally promised not to do it again for the balance of her school career. Now I discovered that she has done it again with a fellow student.

She wants to move out, but we don't let her. We trusted her all these years, and while we were abroad for a while, she probably succumbed for the first time.

What can perplexed parents do in such a case to straighten out the mess?

ANSWER: The promiscuous female, like the Don Juan, is a wandering soul in search of the love and true acceptance which she never felt she had gotten in her home from her parents. Because the motivation for their behavior is to search for love, while not really able to give it, they never find what they are looking for.

The Don Juan never finds complete satisfaction with a woman, for what he unconsciously really wants a woman cannot give him, for only a man has it. The promiscuous female is searching for a male, but one who is also unacceptable for another reason. She is looking for a father in each man with whom she is intimate, because she never felt sufficiently close to and loved by her real father.

This sometimes happens because the mother stands between the father and the daughter, and is as jealous of the young daughter as an older sister would be of a younger one. Perhaps your daughter was taken for granted and emotionally neglected because she was the second female in the family and the one who came last. She may have been a disappointment because she did not turn out to be the little boy whom the parents, particularly the mother, wanted.

You may be right that she started this flirting when you were abroad. But your prolonged absence and greater geographical distance from her only brought her loneliness and her feeling of exclusion to a head. It merely precipitated behavior that was long in the making.

It is not clear just what you consider to be the "mess." Is it your disappointment in your daughter and your shame, or the fact that her promiscuity came to your attention, and therefore, presented you with a mess, or is it a deep concern for a troubled child who happens to be yours?

The solution which you evidently found satisfactory was to make your daughter promise not to do it again for the balance of her school career. What she may conclude you are saying to her is that this behavior is frowned upon while she is a college student because of the danger of being caught by the authorities and expelled. However, if she is a good girl as long as she remains in school, she can do anything she wants once she has graduated. The promise you elicited from her was therefore really a compromise in which you were giving her permission to do anything she wanted, with as many men as she wanted, once she had finished school.

If this compromise is typical of compromises made with her through her growing years, then it is understandable why she has not developed a strong enough conscience to say no to impulses that she knows will do her more harm than good. One cannot teach long-term values by making a short-term verbal contract like this. It is more helpful to try to discover why she has this need to give herself to many. Perhaps it is in order to feel that she is wanted. Then, maybe she will be chosen by the right man for her, some day.

This has probably seemed to her another evidence of how little her parents care about her. Her threat to move out is intended only to cause you to beg her to stay. If, after learning all this about her and disapproving of what you found out, you still can't bring yourselves to put her out, she concludes that you must care about her.

Whatever the sources of your information, whether it was from her older sister, from a friend, or from clues, like letters which she left around for you to see and read, you can be sure that your daughter wanted you to know and wanted to be found out. Unable to control herself in the first place, and then failing later to keep her promise that she would do so, she needed to be discovered in order to be helped.

She is calling to you to rescue her and to provide help for her. Then she will be able to help herself and not repeat the behavior of which, you may be sure, she is not particularly proud. Asking a weak person to promise to be strong, is like asking a sinking man to promise not to drown.

In a peaceful and serious family conference, in which your love, rather than your disapproval, should set the tone, you should suggest to your daughter that she go for analytic therapy. This would help her to get some insights not only into her behavior, but also into the reasons why she wants to be caught. If she leaves clues all over the place, she obviously wants to be discovered so as to have her impulses kept under control.

Your daughter is not a bad girl, but a troubled human being who needs help. If she sees that you are willing to do everything humanly possible to help her find peace within herself, she will make peace with her parents. Then, ultimately, she will be able to find one man, all her own.

When they found their own family, you will be an integral part of it and will share its joys.

2. BUDDING ADULTS AND BEWILDERED PARENTS

The saying goes that people are known by the company they keep. In the same vein, Middle Generation parents are often known by the problems they encounter. In this age group, parents may have to contend with both married and unmarried children.

Let's take a look at what goes on between these same parents and their dependent children.

Broadly speaking, these dependent children fall into three main groups: early teenagers; those in their late teens, on the threshold of adulthood; and young adults who have not yet left the parental home to build families of their own. Each group faces problems peculiar to its physical age and its stage of emotional development, and reacts and evokes reactions to and from the parents in distinctive ways.

To the parents, the range of problems they find themselves faced with seems to be wider and increasingly difficult. Developing personalities demand latitude for their self-expression. Old-established standards of personal conduct within the home suddenly collapse. The natural rebelliousness of the adolescent goes out of its way to stage confrontations with the natural corrective and protective instincts of the parent. Relationships formed outside the family circle take on alarming proportions and exert untoward influence. The child seems poised to fly away before his wings are strong enough to carry him.

Or, the reverse seems to be the case. The youngster doesn't seem to want to fly at all. The boy clings to the nest stubbornly. His contacts with the opposite sex are either nonexistent or unrealistic. The girl won't date. She doesn't go out with anyone and has her nose stuck in a book all the time.

What concerns the parents most of all is the transformation going on in the parent-child relationship. Often the child is well aware of it and goes out of his way to force the issue. It takes time for some parents to realize that the maturing process their children are experiencing calls for a corresponding maturing of their own attitudes and relations with the child. They must adjust to the fact that in the not too distant future, the relationship, if it is to be a lasting one, will have to be transmuted into one between two adults, instead of between child and parent. The Sixty-Four Dollar Question is how to recognize and handle it when that time has arrived.

I

Adolescent rebellion does not usually emerge full-blown. Its first shoots usually appear during the pre-teen years, and by the time the youngster is in his early teens, it begins to flower openly.

Very often it uses as its vehicle some popular fad or movement that has caught on with the young generation, like hair, in the letter below. From the parents' viewpoint, it may seem outlandish and even alarming, particularly if it has connotations of anti-social behavior. This is a time for the parents to strive for a balanced perspective, and not to push the panic button.

LETTER: *Our son, fourteen, is a freshman in a private high school of very high standing. In the past few months, we have noticed a distinct change in him. He has become engrossed with the "Hippies."*

I know that many teenagers are interested and intrigued by this movement. However, he thinks about it too much and looks upon himself as a pseudo-hippie. He even purchased psychedelic glasses and buttons.

We decided to become more firm with him, and as an initial step, insisted that he trim his hair. It was not too long, but looked sloppy. Besides, this particular style did not make him look attractive.

His grades in school are beginning to suffer and he is in a constant state of fear that he might not pass. He is the eldest of three brothers, the others being six and nine. They are good students and do their assignments without any prodding from us. He insists he wishes to attend college, but we tell him that with these grades this may not be possible.

How can we motivate him to put more effort into study?

ANSWER: The psychological phenomenon of rebelliousness has always been characteristic of adolescence. The way this rebelliousness has been acted out has, of course, differed from generation to generation. But the modes of expression, whether in dress or behavior, take on the garb of the times, and so stay in fashion.

The long hair of today may become unfashionable

What can I do without hurting anybody?

ANSWER: During adolescence when the youngster is in the process of finding himself, he will always find himself wanting in some areas.

To build himself up he will belittle the parent in his thoughts or fantasies. Since even the most loving, mature and aware parents will err sometimes in the way they handle their child or manage a difficult situation, the youngster is not fantasying when he points to errors they have made. Nevertheless, deep down, although he bitterly resents it when they demand perfection of him, he still wants them to be perfect.

When parents do things for relatives with whom the youngster has a good and close relationship, he will not resent it as much. But when the youngster is not close to the relatives, he sees them as siblings with whom he has to compete for his parents' bounty and love.

You feel that advantage was taken of your father at a great disadvantage to you. You reason that your father should have found some way of getting all the brothers and sisters to be equally helpful and mindful of their parents and match his contribution.

On the other hand, they may have reasoned that he was staying so close to his parents only because he wanted to take over the family business. So, to them, your father was not really deprived, but the favored son in whom their parents had the greatest trust and faith.

Perhaps it is some of these accusations which you may have overheard that made you think that the business is more important to your father than you, his son, and that his mother is more important to him than his wife, your mother.

The fact that you can express the kind of feelings you

do, and say how much you missed having a closer relationship with your father indicates that basically the relationship is one of mutual love.

Your father may be a little sad to be told how deprived you felt. However, he will also be very proud of you, and of the fact that you can speak up for yourself. He will no doubt try to change his schedule so that you can be together more. Thus, you will do a lot for your father, and be as good a son to him as he was to his parents in his own way.

III

Mothers and adolescent daughters also develop a very special quality in their relationship during these years. Usually, the mother expects her daughter to live up to certain standards and respect certain values that she has established in her home.

A mother expects help with her chores around the house. To her they may represent keeping up a standard. But to a girl in her late teens, they often represent a special hurdle and sometimes an imposition. Behind her attitude may be the youngster's need to make a move toward independence, and refusing to do chores may be the form it takes.

The spirit of outright rebellion, as this mother found, is sparked by many underlying factors, some open and direct, but others relating to the young adolescent girl's basic need for self-approval and self-appreciation.

If she doesn't get approval at home, she may either feel she doesn't deserve it at all and withdraw from the scene, or else try to get it wherever she can.

LETTER: *We are in our middle forties and happily married. My husband has a successful business, and I work in his office five hours every day.*

We have a girl seventeen, and a boy thirteen. The girl, a high-school senior, is an honor student. She is very attractive and very popular with both boys and girls. She is constantly at her friends' homes, but rarely brings her friends home.

She is extremely clean about her person, her room, and her possessions. However, the rest of the house doesn't matter with her. She does the household chores with resentment and many objections. The chores are never done properly, and I must call her back to finish what was left undone. We now find it difficult to talk with her. She gets extremely angry at the slightest disagreement.

I was not feeling well some weeks ago, and she showed no concern whatsoever. When her brother was ill, she was disgusted at the attention I gave him. However, when she is ill, I show great concern.

She had a summer job and banked her entire salary, which she will need during college.

ANSWER: As a little one, every girl sees in her mother the ideal of what she herself wants to be. But, in adolescence, to hold onto this would make her too dependent on her parents and too fearful of letting go. As a result of this drive to break away, it often happens that nothing the mother says is acceptable to the child.

Youngsters love to bring their friends to their homes when they can show off, not the affluence and mode of living, but the good relationship they have with their parents and the respect they get from them.

A girl who feels that her mother is more concerned about her own appearance and how attractive she is, or that she wants to be "one of the girls" with her daughter's friends, will not want to expose herself to such an atmosphere. Just as the mother wants her growing daughter to act her age, so the daughter wants her mother to act her age and behave like a mother, not like a "pal."

You work in your husband's office for five hours a day, evidently not out of need but for the gratification that you get from it. But you also evidently ask your daughter to take on some of the household chores which you as a mother would assume if you were not working. She then feels imposed upon.

A girl like your daughter would no doubt be considerate and mindful of your needs if she weren't made to feel that, in order to be a good daughter, she has to be motherly to her own mother. It is part of every mother's duty to take care of her children in their growing years. To equate your care of her with her care of you is not to make her your equal, but to ask too much of her, when she feels she is not getting enough from you.

When your daughter takes good care of her room and her possessions and in addition saves her earnings for her college years, she is showing a high degree of responsibility and maturity. What she wants to hear from you is praise and approval for her very responsible behavior, not a catalogue of what she hasn't done or hasn't done well enough.

IV

One of the worst experiences any child can go through is that of actually being rejected by a parent, or getting the feeling that he or she is. This threatens not only his sense of security, but his very existence as a member of the family.

The young man described below is tormented by a disturbing question: was he really wanted? The answer he dreads bears down on him harder and harder as he gets older. By the time he stands on the verge of manhood, it can become obsessing, no matter how well he contends with his other problems.

LETTER: *We have a boy of eighteen, handsome, charming, and well-liked, and also high strung. He is a college sophomore.*

He has a very high IQ. In elementary school he won the medal for highest scholarship and good citizenship. He was also the most popular boy in school.

He was sent to a school in a tough neighborhood that had a class for gifted children. The principal announced in the assembly that he was the foremost pupil in the school.

After that, several pupils waylaid him. He handled the situation himself; made friends with the nicer ones and became "one of the boys." His marks became average— and have remained so. It is as though he decided it didn't pay to be better than average.

Since he was nine, he worked after school and weekends selling papers, shining shoes, etc. At seventeen, he had saved $1,000. He started to buy his own clothes, pay for his dating, and bought a hi-fi set. Before long the money was spent. When scolded he said the money was his.

My husband, an attorney, is an impatient man. When displeased he asks the boy to leave home. (When the boy was three, his father left home, saying he was in love with someone else. We were reconciled after six years. But he is always ready to talk divorce or separation in a disagreement or when he is displeased.)

Last summer he worked at a summer resort. We learned the boy was smoking. We are both sensitive to smoke and very much against it. My husband again told him he can't come home, but apologized afterward.

My son can't sleep. Since last summer he stays up

nights. When he retires earlier, he reads or gets up and goes for a walk. He has been looking for a job spasmodically. He has been late for classes twice.

The boy tells me he can't tolerate the knowledge that his father doesn't want him. The father says he can't stand the boy's staying up nights, and his lack of respect. He feels the only way to deal with the boy is to be "tough."

ANSWER: As hard a time as you have with the ups and downs of your marriage, and your efforts to keep the family together, this is almost nothing compared to what your son goes through.

At the time of the departure of your husband, your son was but three and unable to understand intellectually what was going on. Emotionally, however, he understood all the uncertainties of feeling and the clashes that were taking place around him. By the time his father returned, more of the meaning of what had taken place during his early childhood became clear to him.

From your devotion to him, and because he wanted to prove to you that he was a dependable male, he gained the strength to put all his natural endowments of mind and body to work. He did not miss the connection between his beginning to work and his father's return home after a long absence. He hoped that his success at school and his conscientiousness about work and money would prove that he was a good boy, and make him more acceptable to his father.

When working and striving toward this end did not bring the desired rewards, he began to give to himself what had either not been given to him sufficiently before, or had actually been denied him by his family. The only thing that he felt really belonged to him was the money he had worked for and saved. The clothes, the hi-fi, and the other things which he bought were symbolic gifts of love and appreciation from himself to himself, for which he was starved.

His inability to fall asleep is probably only another manifestation of the same difficulty with which he has felt himself saddled. Daytime hours are not enough for the job of trying to think through his problems and find some workable solution to them all by himself. This is about the hardest assignment anybody his age can undertake. So he also puts in overtime during the night hours—the only free time he has.

The adults in his life continuously scrap with him about minor infractions as if they were major crimes. Whenever he tries to express himself, they seem to be totally against him. His father threatens to expel him every time he is displeased with him. This confirms the boy's worst suspicions about never really having been wanted, and makes him feel that only as long as he is the good, conforming little boy and satisfies all of his parents' demands is his presence accepted.

You, in your own way, are trying to be helpful. However, father and son are treated like two bad boys. Your role of mediator and peacemaker, after the battle, makes both contenders dependent on you and keeps them both feeling somewhat incompetent and childish. One is made to apologize for his wrong-doing, and the other to admit that his wrongs started the fight.

The successes your son achieved in school just didn't pay off. Too much was asked of him, too early, and the rewards were not commensurate with the effort expended. But this alone was not responsible for his lowered marks in school. Until he is able to get closer to his father, he will remain too worn-out emotionally to produce. He cannot do so when he is kept under continuous scrutiny, with the threat of being dispossessed constantly held over his head.

Although he had stayed with his mother through

thick and thin, while his father deserted her, when he returned, your son had to give up his special role and status. Your husband returned to you, but he did not return to the boy, and this made the boy feel like a two-time loser.

Your husband should examine why he uses the threat of leaving to build up his own self-esteem. Perhaps he is hard on his child because he feels life has been hard on him. But who better than he should know that toughness does not pay off.

He evidently has traits and characteristics which are found lovable and desirable by others. If he could accept these, he could then become more accepting of his child.

Therapy might help him to become more of his own man. Perhaps the final step in his return home is his reconciliation with his own son.

V

Rebellious teenagers are as natural as snow and rain. It's all part of growing up and should be appreciated as such by the parents.

When a teenager, however, goes out of her way to disregard or overturn basic family values and teachings, then it is time for the parents to sit up and take notice. The first step may be, not to criticize and punish, but to listen to what she is trying to tell them. Evidently this girl had a message which her parents did not hear.

LETTER: *My two older daughters are very happily married and we have three wonderful grandchildren whom my husband and I adore. They have always been good children and I have never had any trouble with them as far as their going out of their way to do things that would hurt my husband or myself. Now my youngest daughter, almost eighteen, is doing just that.*

She is going with a boy who is not of our religion and there is nothing I can say or do that will discourage her from seeing him. I've tried to punish her by not letting her go out, and that has only made her lie about where she was going. One day I caught her in this lie and she became so furious that the next day when I was out, she ran away from home saying that she was sick and tired of my telling her what to do and not trusting her.

They both went to this boy's aunt's place, stayed there overnight. She came home the next day. When I reprimanded her for this she said she wasn't going to marry him. But in the meantime, she doesn't see anybody else. When I try to tell her she is not doing the right thing, she flares up and refuses to listen. The atmosphere is very unpleasant in our home. She doesn't talk to us or even to her sisters when they come to visit. We are heartsick about the whole thing.

ANSWER: Sometimes if parents had planned deliberately to throw their daughter right into the arms of a boy, they could not have been more successful than by what they do to stop it.

Girls, like boys, when they are exploring to find out what kind of mate they will want, make attachments that are obviously not really for them. They look for something different in the other, to satisfy their wish to be unusual and outstanding themselves.

When parents take it personally, as a repudiation of them and their teachings, the child, in turn, sees it as a repudiation of what she is and hopes to be. A parent-child war then develops which has little or nothing to do with the inner conflict which the child is trying to work out. Because the battle is now out in the open, the youngster begins to think that the relationship with her parents is really the basis of all her troubles. She then looks to an outsider, usually to the boy of the moment, to rescue her.

As the youngest in the family, this daughter had more attention and more older people to give it to her, than your first two daughters. When her two sisters got married, she was glad to see them go because now she could be the one and only. Also since she was the oldest left at home, she could now enjoy both the emoluments of being the baby and those of being grown up.

When the grandchildren came, the love and adoration which her parents showered on them made them her competitors. But as an aunt, she was also supposed to shower these babies with affection and attention, which she could not feel.

From being the hub of the wheel around which the whole world revolved, she suddenly felt like an outsider. And as such, she looked for someone outside the familial orbit to hold onto.

She felt she owed you no obedience because you took away from her what she coveted most—her status, when you displaced her by having other babies in the house.

An eighteen-year-old girl cannot be treated like a baby whose every move must be watched and closely supervised. A youngster must be given trust, if she is to be trustworthy. Then she will maintain trust in the faith and values of her parents. The mistakes children make while testing their parents' teachings to see which they can live comfortably with, need only be passing errors. When the parents magnify them into life-and-death issues, it warps the child's judgment.

Your daughter may have been driven into lying because she felt you lied to her when you said you trusted her. Your deeds contradicted your words. She perhaps did not want to vent her anger on her parents for making her feel like such a bad daughter after being told how she was hurting them. Running away even for one night may have meant running away from the guilt which this provoked.

She does not talk to her parents or her sisters because she may feel they are all aligned against her. They listen with unfriendly ears and mark her wrong before she has a chance to finish. Since she can never be right with them, she feels they have forfeited her confidences.

It will not help to tell her again that you believe her and have confidence in her. The only way is to let her manage her own social life. She will ask for any advice or counsel she may want and you should not offer it until she does so.

Overly strict and inappropriate discipline will only push her into doing what you are so set against. When she is free to come and go, she will feel free to return to the bosom of the family. She needs confidence that you will like and find acceptable any friends she makes.

VI

Youngsters who don't seem to be attracted to the opposite sex, especially when they are of an age when their friends are already so involved, are usually sources of worry and concern for their parents. However, sometimes it is hard to define exactly what the parent is really concerned about. Is it possible spinsterhood or bachelorhood for the child? Or is it something that really has more to do with the parent than the child? Is it something like this mother's question?

LETTER: *How can I get peace of mind and overcome my feelings of depression?*

My eighteen-year-old daughter, away at a nearby college, has never dated a boy who has called her. Occasionally, someone will "fix her up," but it doesn't happen often.

She is very pretty, dresses well, is popular with girls and has many friends. She finds outlets in the theater and in the arts.

At this age she is missing fun and the emotional security and good feeling that come with dating. I find myself thinking about this constantly and hoping for a miracle. My husband doesn't like to talk about it.

We have an older boy who is doing extremely well in college and is getting married to a lovely girl in two months.

ANSWER: When a daughter is not popular and doesn't make or maintain friendships easily, the mother may feel critical of her. But deep down, she may feel that somehow she herself was responsible.

In early childhood, the girl wants the mother out of the way, so that she can have her father all to herself. Later, the situation is reversed. The mother wants the daughter married, and out of the way, so that she can once again have her husband's exclusive attention. When a daughter stays unmarried, the mother is plagued by guilt over this, and feels she may have stood in the way of her emotional development.

Some youngsters are late bloomers socially, just as there are some who are late bloomers intellectually. Some can handle only one area of adjustment at a time. They will first work very hard at school, and only after having established themselves scholastically will they begin to give attention to the social area. Others feel they must establish themselves socially, in relationships with the opposite sex, before they can apply themselves seriously to schoolwork.

With as many friends as your daughter has, there is no need to worry about this. It may take her a little longer before she begins to date, but the time cannot be too far off.

Perhaps it is hard for you to give up your boy to another female, however much you like the girl. That your daughter is late in dating may point up your feeling that it is early for your son to get married. Depression is often caused by hostility which a person cannot express against others and turns inward upon herself. Your depression may really be caused by unreadiness to relinquish your son to another, resulting in hostility to him and his future wife. It could hurt your daughter's social adjustment to make her feel responsible for your depression. She might also size up the situation as more hopeless than it is.

Direct your attention and energies to the happy event about to take place, and let your daughter participate and contribute to the plans for the wedding parties and celebrations. When you are able to give up your son willingly and graciously, your daughter will be able to emerge and not feel that she is hurting you by not falling in love on schedule.

VII

It is not only children who overreact. Parents do too, particularly when they are convinced that what they are doing is right for their child.

The older a child gets, however, the more attention parents have to pay to their own motives. An older daughter who has passed the age of consent does not need the kind of guidance this father insisted upon. She needs, instead, the quality of trust and confidence that would make her feel competent as well as appreciated and loved.

Conflict between parents as to what is right does not help, but can only confuse the situation, and the youngster.

LETTER: *I have a daughter nineteen who works and contributes to her upkeep. My wife worships the ground she walks on, and very seldom sides with me when I try to talk to my daughter about her continuous late hours and my feelings about some of her friends. My wife pays much more attention to my daughter than she does to me.*

I realize that independence means a lot to these young people, but as a father, I feel it my duty and responsibility to try to guide her on the right road. I feel especially strong on this point, as I have inadvertently caught her on two occasions involved in necking with the same boy in our living room.

It is impossible to talk to my daughter. It is also out of the question to talk to her number one fan, namely, my wife. How do I get through? I don't see my daughter too often. She also attends college at night.

ANSWER: Inconsistency in the attitudes and behavior of parents is what youngsters complain about most. While parents want the growing youngster to take on responsibilities, at the same time she is expected to be wholly dependent on the parents' decisions as to what to do, with whom to associate, and how to set her daily routines and plan her future life.

Some youngsters will take this because, while fighting for independence, they cannot let go of the parents, whom they still need so much. But when the young person begins carrying out her responsibilities in a conscientious and reliable way, over-concern on the part of the parents no longer is seen as a sign of love. Rather it says that they expect the worst of her.

Perhaps you are trying so hard to become involved

again in your daughter's life because you pushed her into going to work and paying for her keep, when there was no need for either. However, for her to have gone to college during the day might have meant being entirely subservient to your commands, without any freedom to spend her time the way she wanted to.

Hugging and kissing between two youngsters who like each other, does not necessarily lead to heavy petting or sexual intimacy. Mindful of each other, they do not make excessive demands.

That your daughter brought her boyfriend into your home should make you feel secure. Usually, youngsters who want to go too far go to a place far away from home.

Before your daughter will listen to you as a father and accept your guidance, she must first see you acting as a loving husband and reestablishing the good and close relationship you had with her mother. A husband who is mindful, respectful and appreciative of his wife, sets up the image of the kind of man his daughter will want in marriage. She will relate only to someone who is as protective of her as her father is of her mother. When you go back to your wife, your daughter will come back to you.

VIII

Every once in a while, we come across a reverse kind of relationship in which a young person seeks a parent figure as his love object. Love for a parent, good as it seems to be while a child is growing up, may actually be harmful if excessive and if prolonged beyond its appropriate time.

If the condition is not corrected, the result is a chronically immature individual, who still seeks to be a favorite child to his parents at an age when he should be able to function independently. If he is able to cut "the silver cord," it may only be to marry an older woman, and thus find a mother to feed and pamper him again. It is a Middle Generation problem in that he does not want a younger generation mate, but will only accept one from the Middle Generation.

Parents with a son who has the problem described below, become painfully aware of their guilty feelings. They believe they are in some way responsible for it. They then begin the painful process of digging into the past to uncover what led to their son's strange choice of life-companion.

LETTER: *We have a son who is twenty-five years old.*

He does not seem to like young girls. He feels most comfortable with elderly women. He does not take girls out, except when he thinks it is necessary to make a show.

What shall we do?

ANSWER: When a young man is twenty-five and his mother (or father, for that matter) still worries about his dates, he cannot be regarded as of age emotionally. It is often found that his parents have kept him from moving forward and developing on his own. This parental control and management is more apparent, usually, in the case of a girl.

From his experience at home, your son has learned that an older woman hovers over him, takes care of him, and expects little from him in return. He probably enjoys being treated like a bright and good little boy who receives approval for everything he says or does.

Older women are proud and grateful for having a young man seek them out. He is not required to take total charge of any situation, like a mature man, but he can be manipulated and controlled as a mother does with her little boy. Yet he can protect himself this way from becoming serious with a young female, which would force an unwelcome role on him. Dating a young girl would pose a threat to the life he is now leading. He therefore sees in a young girl more a sibling than a date.

This shows that he is not ready for marriage. He probably wants to avoid it like the plague. By paying attention to other elderly women, he distracts his father from discovering how much he still wants his mother. Also, he says to his mother by his actions, what he cannot possibly say in words—that she is still the most desirable woman in his life.

An older woman who is almost old enough to be a mother to the male she marries, gets a son along with a husband. Paradoxically, even great differences in age, background, education, belief, and the like, can be exactly what makes a good relationship possible between such a couple. They meet the other's basic needs. As long as they continue to do so, the marriage can last.

Sometimes, however, after they have been married for a while, and these deep-seated desires have obtained some satisfaction, one or both of them may develop a strong urge to become single again. They will then find a new mate who matches their new level of development.

In some family relationships, the mother takes over. Subtly and circuitously, she plays her husband off against her son. These are the two men in her life, her two lovers.

Once your husband takes over as the man of the house, it will help your son grow into mature manhood. He will then "act his age," and date girls his own age.

✒ 3. ON BECOMING AN IN-LAW

Some parents expect their children to change over night because they are married. The newlyweds are supposed to settle down and behave like old married people. They are no longer thought of as children, but as adults who have finally demonstrated, by getting married, that they are prepared to take on in full the responsibilities of life. Yet, at the same time, certain things are supposed to remain as they were before the marriage. The parents still think of themselves as parents. The married adult is still their child, so the old lines of authority are supposed to remain intact.

Some married children subscribe to these ideas to a surprising extent. They want certain benefits of their former lives as dependent children to carry over into their lives as independent adults. Conflicts arise when these are not forthcoming. They are often reflections of the old battles of parent-child relationships. Father-daughter, mother-son ties fray and threaten to come apart, and the old rebellions flare up again. The daughter-in-law revives her old anti-mother campaign against her husband's mother. The husband insists that his bride pledge complete allegiance to the new loyalty and give up the old.

The problems are varied, but they all express a common need to adjust to growth. Ultimately, "the silver cord" is replaced by a more flexible attachment, one that allows the expanded family unit to breathe and find itself, while the old relationships are fitted to the new way of life.

I

The wedding is over. The honeymoon is a thing of the past. The new day that dawned for both parents and newlyweds has advanced toward noon. It is now apparent that no one was completely prepared for the new circumstances. The flight of the fledgling from the nest can never be gradual enough.

The period of adjustment may be easy enough for the newlyweds who have the fun and excitement of building a new life with the new and exciting partner at their sides. Their parents, however, are faced with the necessity of altering old living patterns that have developed over many years. The Middle Generation has to learn the lesson that all must ultimately face when the threshold of middle age is reached. They must learn how to live in their home without the child who is now married—something they have not experienced since the early days of their own marriage. For them it is as much a new situation as it is for the newlyweds, and it is, perhaps, a little more difficult, as this mother-of-the-groom has found:

LETTER: *What has happened to the warm, friendly relationship between parents and their children?*

Our son, an only child, married a very lovely girl and we looked forward to a happy addition to our little family circle. It is only a short time after their marriage, but little by little, the children visit us less and less often. They never see us over the weekends. They live only thirty minutes away from us.

Lately, my son visits us for a short time, alone, and offers some flimsy excuse for his wife's absence. We have always treated the children with greatest respect, affection, attention, consideration and "hands off" policy. There is no reason for this estrangement and we are very upset by their behavior.

Where have we as parents gone wrong? Should we ask them for an explanation?

ANSWER: Even when the most cherished dream of life has come to pass and the "one and only" has been found and the couple are joined together in love and marriage, there is always a period of adjustment following the union. The change from the old to a new way of life while getting to know each other better takes time.

But it is not only the young couple that have to adjust. The parents of the young marrieds, too, have to learn to live apart from them, even as they have to learn all over again how to live together without their child.

During this period of readjustment some parents-in-law become very critical of the newcomer in the family. They may express this openly to their child or to the new in-law. But sometimes they express it through uncalled-for suggestions as to what and how things should be done. They rationalize that they are only informing their child's new mate about the way of living to which their child has been accustomed.

The young spouse feels this as an intrusion and takes it as an expression of lack of confidence and respect for her. She then reacts by removing herself from the in-laws.

Sometimes the break is due to the young bride's relationship with her own mother. Angers and resentments for the hurts and deprivations her parents visited upon her, which she was never able to express, she now takes out on her mother-in-law. By finding a substitute target, she can continue to feel that she is a good daughter. The married son who felt it would have been ingratitude to his parents to rebel, now lets his wife do it for him.

However, no matter how respectful and mindful the parents and parents-in-law are during the first years of the young couple's marriage, they want and need to be by themselves, away from the family. In addition to their intimate person-to-person adjustment, there is a realignment and screening of the friends that each of them had before marriage.

In addition, the young pair want to make new friends. This is done on a different basis with the education, background and interests of both partners, as well as the work associates of the husband, as the basic screening measures. It is best for the young marrieds to be with each other alone as much as possible, particularly over the weekends, when their time is their own.

In any good family relationship, an honest and kindly presentation of a problem usually leads to the best solution. To discuss some of the misinterpretations that could have taken place, and also some of the acts of commission and omission that were found objectionable, can often help. It is not a "hands-off" policy that the young people want basically. They want to be given time and respect. Then, when they extend their hand in loving consideration, and are not made to feel guilty for not having done it at the time desired by the in-laws, a good relationship can be established.

II

Usually the things that upset the relations between Middle Generationites and their married children are very specific. When an only child marries, for instance, who will fill the void in the parents' lives? Most mothers and daughters can and often do get along. However, if the daughter is an only child, the relationship takes on oversized proportions for one or the other. If the mother has depended on her daughter to make up for the lack of other children or to compensate for the lack of other interests in her life, the daughter's marriage inevitably puts a strain on the relationship. The daughter finds herself enjoying a new sense of freedom, but her mother finds herself unaccustomedly thrown back on her own resources. How well can this mother, who writes the following letter, survive being alone?

LETTER: *My daughter, twenty, an only child, married two and a half years ago and lives in a city close by. We have always had a tremendously close relationship.*

During her adolescence we quarreled like mad. She was fresh, disobedient about curfews, etc., but it made no difference in our love for each other. We are both interested in civil rights, poetry, analysis of our motives, and our relationship with each other.

However, her husband is extremely jealous of our relationship. Now, I see her infrequently—every two or three weeks—and this winter when I lived down South I saw her only twice.

She consulted an expert who told her that she was too attached to me and we must "give each other up." How do you stop a twenty-year relationship of love? I call when her husband is not around. We are not natural with each other any more—polite but strange.

My son-in-law is very fond of my husband, whose attitude toward our daughter is very different. He loves her, but he is not interested in what she thinks or does, so he is no threat to my son-in-law.

ANSWER: An only child is often a lonely child, but almost as often, the mother of an only child feels isolated and alone. When she goes off with friends or engages in activities leaving her child alone, she feels guilty. As a result, such mothers take their children with them wherever they go. They expect their friends to behave like additional parents or siblings to their little ones. As a youngster becomes older, the parent tries to include her in her adult activities, and treats her as one of the crowd.

However, being included in the world of adults before she has reached adulthood is not an advantage for the youngster. She feels the parent's love as a too-great attachment and dependence on her. When a mother becomes the daughter's best friend, it keeps the daughter from having best friends her own age or bringing her peers into her home.

The daughter inevitably sees her mother as a competitor and a rival, and the mother all too often gives the youngster grounds for this attitude. At parties, such a mother may socialize with the youngsters and act like one of the crowd to show how "in" she is. The daughter feels that she can never win out against such an attractive and experienced female.

Your daughter's husband, by standing up for his rights and for their right to build a life on their own as a couple, is perhaps talking both for himself and his wife's father. He is telling you that the proper person with whom your interests should be shared is your husband.

The fact that your daughter married so young may be an indication that she had to get away from you and your mutual dependence in order to be a person in her own right.

It is not jealousy, but love for his wife that gave her husband the strength to fight for her liberation. You are not being asked to break with your daughter, but rather to break away from your dependence on her, so that a good and healthy mother-daughter relationship can be established. Your daughter wants the freedom to grow on her own at her husband's side, as his wife and the mother of his children, rather than as your ever-loving bosom companion. Your son-in-law is well within his rights when he doesn't want to have to compete with you for the love of his wife.

There are women your age everywhere who are interested in the arts, who work for causes, who help the underprivileged or handicapped. These are the people with whom you should associate.

When you and your husband have built a life of your own, you will not call on your daughter to fill all the voids in your life which now exist. She and her husband will then welcome you into their home and will enjoy spending time with you.

This cannot help but improve the relationship and allow it to settle into a proper mother-daughter and mother-in-law son-in-law pattern, without the jealousies and hostilities which now plague all of you.

III

In the mother-daughter relationship depicted here, the parent's dependence on the married child produced a sad and surprising reaction. The fear of death is not always what it seems. The healthy reaction of the single sibling, by contrast, underlines the problem.

LETTER: *I am a very troubled mother of two girls, eighteen and twenty-three. I realize children are greatly influenced by a mother's attitudes and expressions, but we are not always aware of this at the time we are rearing them.*

My husband and I do not get along, although we go everywhere together. We never quarrel verbally, but the constant silence is worse.

My older girl has been married three years. She is in her sixth month of pregnancy. Ever since she became pregnant, she is obsessed with the fear of dying. This daughter is extremely attached to me, and also fears my dying. She is afraid of being left alone.

My younger daughter is very distant and does not confide in me. I try to draw her out, but she resents it. My husband is an extreme introvert, and I am an extreme extrovert.

How have I failed? Was it the extreme silence between my husband and myself?

ANSWER: With the best of intentions, every parent makes some mistakes. Even when no mistake has really been made, misinterpretation of the parent's attitudes or actions can create problems for the child. With time and maturity such problems become more or less resolved, and the person can go on to build a new life of her own.

Especially if the parent recognizes that a mistake has been made and goes about remedying the situation, she has not really failed.

To fill up the void created by the silence between your husband and yourself, you probably made your children the center of your life and interest. This gave you a reason for existence and a status in life. The married daughter's overattachment to you may have come from your dependence on her.

While children appreciate the overdedicated mother during their younger years, they resent and rebel against her in their later years. But when the mother has "given her all," like a saint or a martyr, they cannot rebel without feeling terribly guilty. The child permits the mother to hold onto her, and suppresses all the normal resentments and hostilities.

Unfortunately, such suppression makes these hostilities accumulate and grow. The fear that these feelings will be discovered or will actually be powerful enough to have the secretly wished-for effect upsets the individual. The preoccupation with death is basically a consequence of this hostility. In fearing her own death, the person turns this hostility inward upon herself, in punishment.

Your daughter's fear of being left alone may be her way of telling you to leave her alone. Her obstetrician is, in all probability, aware of the situation. Sometimes an obstetrician can help a mother-to-be to see that she really wants to become a parent. If more help is needed, he will make the referral.

Your younger daughter is reacting normally and healthily in not making you her confidante, or wanting to be yours. At this age, if she needs someone in whom to confide it should be a friend or her older sister, not the parent.

Perhaps now that your children are grown, you should begin work on a job long past due, that is, reestablishing communications with your husband. Being the extrovert you say you are, it should be easier for you to make the overtures. Express to him your wish to start talking, emotionally as well as verbally.

Your daughter needs to see that you have regained

your hope and faith and want to rebuild your life with your husband. Then her fears of death, which are really fears of breakups and separations within the family, will diminish and she will give reaffirmation to her love of life and its continuity.

IV

The relationships that develop between parents and their children are never simple. There is much more involved than the basic tie between provider and dependent, much more than the obvious biological fact of parenthood.

This is especially true between parents and children of the opposite sex. The sexual aspects of their relationship are usually too subtle and submerged to be readily detected. They are hardly ever mutually or self-acknowledged. Naturally, there are some highly complicated psychological factors involved, as the following letter illustrates.

LETTER: *My husband is a professional man and we have three nice sons. Two of them are also professionals. The youngest is still going to school.*

Our oldest son, married six years, recently became a father. He is twenty-seven. Although I love him very much, he is always saying things to hurt me. He then goes out of his way to apologize and promises never to hurt my feelings again. I always forgive him, but he seems to take delight in doing it again. He tells me that he does it deliberately, but he really loves me.

I also get insulted when I visit him. His wife is very cool to me. Lately, instead of answering him when he does this, I walk away. He does not like this, and follows me, and we end up with a kiss. I have made up my mind that I

am going to try very hard to ignore annoying remarks. I am
really very proud of him. He made all the honor societies,
etc.

After the last incident he wrote me a note saying "I'm
very sorry about the stupid things I said. I feel awful about
the way you feel about me, and promise that if you decide
to make up, I won't hurt you again. I love you."

ANSWER: By not letting go of her child, even in marriage, a
mother may intrude and transgress on the private life of the
young people. It is as if a third party is always present.

Interestingly, most in-law conflicts center around the
mother of the husband. One reason is that, having made her
son the second man in her life, the mother now wants to
be repaid by being made the second woman in his life. She
is willing to give him up in marriage only because society
frowns on the mother of a son who doesn't marry. But she
wants "in the worst way" to continue to be part of the life
of the young couple. Sometimes she will be overaggressive,
and act like the mother of two young siblings. Or she will
offer too many invitations to the young couple to visit her,
and will feel hurt when not included in their social life.

The wife, the newcomer in the family, naturally resents this. The advantages of having two women in his life
fighting for his love and attention is something that gives
a husband a sense of power and of being wanted. Naturally
he hates to relinquish it.

Teasing and fighting, followed by "making up" is a
kind of wooing that is sometimes indulged in by couples as
a prelude to their lovemaking. It is totally inappropriate in
a mother-son relationship.

This kind of behavior on the part of both of you—
his impertinence, followed by apologies and then kissing and
making up—is outdated. It must surely be very offensive to

his wife and is in all probability responsible for her "cool-ness" to you.

Too, by treating you the way he does in his wife's presence, he may be saying to her that she has nothing to be jealous of. But this may also be his way of asking her to step in and break up the relationship with you, which he cannot do on his own.

In falling for this game you are permitting childish fantasies to be maintained. Either extreme—being hurt or ignoring his ploy as if it never happened—is to fall for it. It gives him an excuse to pursue you until you notice him, accept his regrets and then kiss and make up.

You should, as one grown-up to another, let him know what you think of this kind of behavior. You could admit that you are as responsible as he is for its continua-tion. For him to be a good father to his own son, he has to give up the image of himself as his mother's little boy.

V

All parents like to believe that they seek to further eventual independence for their children, despite the emotional wrench they will all suffer. Some, however, lean over back-wards in this respect, encouraging their children to become too independent at too early an age. Later on they learn, as this couple did, the dangers of "forcing" independence to come on too soon.

LETTER: *My daughter who lives nearby comes in with her husband once in a while and is ready to go in a few minutes.*

On the other hand, my sister whose daughter lives nearby, is more fortunate. Her daughter and son-in-law come over every Sunday to visit with them and every once in a

*while take weekends in the country with them. My sister is
a very bitter and domineering person and her husband is an
egotist of the worst kind.*

*My husband and I mind our own business. We be-
lieve children should become independent and lead their
own lives as soon as possible. However, we are at a loss to
know why we are shunned and set aside unless we are
needed for some purpose.*

ANSWER: When a child is given too many privileges too soon,
and is told she can make up her own mind about things, the
youngster sees it as a lack of interest in her on the part of
her parents. She feels they don't care enough to bother guiding and directing her.

Particularly during adolescence, when the youngster
is going through the characteristic fluctuations of moods,
feelings and desires, she resents having this responsibility
placed upon her. On the surface, she will fight for her freedom, but deep down, she feels, and perhaps rightfully so,
that in important issues the parents should stay with her and
participate more actively in helping her to arrive at decisions.

You and your husband certainly meant well by "minding your own business" and not becoming more involved in
your daughter's interests and concerns. However, she may
feel that you have not visited enough with her psychologically and emotionally during her growing years, or spent
enough time with her physically, before or since. When parents work too hard on minding their own business, their
grown children may feel that the parents' real purpose is to
keep the children from intruding into their lives.

In citing your sister's relationship with her married
daughter, you imply that bad behavior is rewarded and good
is punished. The picture of your sister as bitter and domi-

neering, and of her husband as egotistical could well be determined by your relationship with them as sister to sister and brother-in-law. But to their children, they may appear as good and loving parents with whom they enjoy being.

You do not have to speak up in hurt or anger to remedy the situation. You could certainly tell your daughter and her husband that you love to be with them, and would like to spend more time together. You and your husband might invite them to your home when you entertain or on other special occasions. You might take them out to dinner and to a theater or concert afterward once in a while.

You are evidently able to help her financially when she is in need. Spend some money for good times on sunny days, instead of saving it only for a rainy day.

VI

Usually some attempt is made on the part of either the parents or the married child to set matters right before the disaffection goes too far. But when the worst is realized and a real split occurs, who suffers the most and pays for the broken family ties? How can the gap be spanned in an extreme case like the following?

LETTER: *My youngest daughter got married a year and a half ago to a very nice young man. Before her marriage we had an empty apartment in a small house we own and in which we live. When we offered it to her she refused. I was shocked and asked the reason. She said that her friends had advised her not to be too near us.*

I was very hurt, because I felt we were real friends. We got along wonderfully, shopping together and giving things to each other. After this I changed and became very bitter. She knew how my husband and I would miss her because we loved her very much. We have visited her only six times since her marriage.

My daughter is expecting a baby soon. I recently had another vacancy and when she found out, she came begging for the apartment. This time I refused and was glad to see her cry. The bitterness made me sick and I needed medical care. We missed her terribly, but now it's all over. I asked her coldly if she had gotten permission from her friends to move back.

Was I right or wrong?

ANSWER: It is universally regarded as better whenever possible for a young couple to start their marriage on territory new to both of them and separated from each of their families. With the best will and strongest resolution in the world, parents living with them or too close to such a young couple tend to treat their married offspring as if they were still children in their household, demanding adult conduct along with childish subservience and dutiful respect.

Their advice is felt as interference, while their expectation that the newly married pair will quickly behave like a settled and experienced couple is taken as a criticism and becomes a threat to the marriage.

The young people soon learn how to adhere to each other in love and fidelity in spite of adjustments that sometimes appear critical and unsurmountable to them and to others. It is easier when daily demands on their loyalty and confidence are not made by the parents. While a young girl is learning how to be a good wife, she cannot always be as attentive a daughter as her mother might wish her to be.

A distinction must be made between the wisdom of your daughter's decision and the reason she gave you for arriving at it.

From the love you gave her, your daughter derived the psychological health and strength not to avail herself of your tempting offer. But because of the possessiveness of your love which she resented and from which she felt she had to free herself, she put into the mouths of others what she still did not have the courage to say to you herself.

She may have felt also that your offer was not entirely unselfish, and that you may have wanted her to continue to live nearby as much for your own benefit as for her welfare. This made it easier for her to talk up and refuse you.

A child, even when grown up, needs to feel that her parents' love and backing are unchanging and that even when she has made mistakes or inflicted hurts, it will in no way change their basic attitude toward her.

When a young woman is about to become a mother and is beset by all the uncertainties so characteristic of pregnancy and so worried about the outcome for herself and the child she is carrying, she needs a mother's open arms and loving concern just as much as she did when she was a little child herself. On the threshold of motherhood and in preparation for it she feels a strong need to repair her own mother-daughter relationship.

Your dependency on your daughter for companionship and friendship must have been rather restricting to both of you, otherwise she would not have had to use so much force to sever the bonds. Underneath, you too must have felt that you were asking too much of her emotionally. In depriving yourself of her company by refusing her the apartment, you punished yourself.

As you well perceived, your own bitterness made you sick and not your daughter's behavior. You really don't like your unmotherly feelings, now that you see that your daughter's decision was not a rejection of you but an attempt to emancipate herself.

You, too, are on the threshold of a new life experience, that of grandmotherhood. You should not deprive yourself of the joys of being the mother of a mother in her own right. Neither should you deny yourself, by this unnecessary and childish breach, the joys in store for you from your grandchild.

Whether or not your daughter comes to live in your house is unimportant. She should be welcomed back into the mansion of your love.

VII

When a child, even a married child, gets into trouble and needs help, the parents' natural reaction is to come to the rescue. Usually, the instinct is a good and proper one and should be followed. But sometimes the reaction gets out of hand. Then it could be like hitting a drowning person over the head with a life preserver, as in this case:

LETTER: *My daughter eloped a year and a half ago at eighteen. We knew she was going out with this chap, but never realized it was so serious, as he never came to the house. We were most upset, but since he came from a good family, we accepted the marriage, inviting his entire family, who live out of town, to a big reception.*

She told us she was moving out of town. By accident we found out she was here, miserable, that he was treating her very badly, and that she was pregnant. They planned to put the child out for adoption as soon as it was born. She had decided to leave him. We were horrified, but nothing would change her mind. My husband and I saw the entire thing through financially. After the baby was placed for adoption through the courts, she got a divorce.

Upon her return home she went back to work and to night college. After being divorced four months, she thinks they will remarry, as he promises to be different.

The girl is attractive, intelligent, and has personality. Yet he seems to hold a whip over her.

I told her if she does this again, this time we will not forgive her. Are we doing the right thing? Is she?

ANSWER: Ultimatums to your daughter, or the threat of excommunication from her family will only provide her with another anvil on which to hammer out further her feeling of not belonging or being wanted. This may only send her hurtling into the arms of this man once more. That this young married couple could plan before their child's birth to place it out for adoption and then follow through with this plan afterward would indicate that their feelings for each other were very shallow.

Such individuals are usually incapable of feeling deeply about anything or anybody, least of all about themselves. In giving up the child, they revealed what utter self-rejection they each suffer from and how useless and unworthy they feel about anything they could produce.

Why your daughter is so unfeeling toward herself, or why she needs to operate in secret from her family, letting the results attest her hostility toward them, is something that she should work out with the help of a psychoanalyst. Otherwise, she may continue helplessly to carry on this program of self-punishment.

Parents always feel that it is basically their fault when children get into trouble. The guilt sometimes puts them on the defensive and they engage their energies in justifying themselves, either finding a culprit to blame or self-righteously exhorting or punishing their child. This is a wasteful dissipation of the concern they really have for their offspring.

Keep the door open for your daughter's return to herself and her family by helping her to achieve emotional stability through treatment. This young man cannot be blamed any more than your daughter. For some reason the unstable emotional needs of each attracted them to each other. These need to be examined and corrected, if they are to have a better life, together or apart.

4. THE DARLING (OR DEMON) YOUR CHILD MARRIED

The relations between parents and the men and women who marry their children often stem from what goes on within their own families. Possessive mothers and fathers tend to regard their sons-and-daughters-in-law as rivals for their children's affections. Authoritarian parents may expect from their child's spouse a measure of the same respect and obedience shown to them by their own son or daughter. Easygoing mothers and fathers who were "pals" to their kids, try to bridge the generation gap between themselves and their new in-laws by the same technique. All parents expect their son-in-law to support their daughter in the style to which they have accustomed her, and if possible, better. Daughters-in-law are expected to enhance the family scene with grace, beauty and womanly accomplishments.

These general attitudes which were so true of past generations of parents, seem still to apply to a surprising extent to contemporary Middle Generation parents. However, parents today display a generally more relaxed attitude toward their children's mates, which in itself results from the almost universal relaxation of traditional parent-child relationships. In our society, it is the rare young man or woman who asks his or her parents' permission to become engaged or get married. These matters are left largely to the children to decide. Unless the parents have strenuous objections to their child's choice of a mate, they will go along with it, regardless of minor misgivings or apprehensions, which they may express privately only among themselves.

It is during the period of adjustment following the happy wedding scene that the problems usually crop up. All sorts of second thoughts drift to the surface, as hitherto unsuspected traits of character and strange behavior show up in the beloved child's spouse. The mother wonders how well the young and inexperienced daughter-in-law is taking care of the precious son. The father worries about whether or not his son-in-law is showing his darling daughter all the love, tenderness and kindness that she deserves. All mothers and fathers are concerned about how well they and the new in-laws will relate to each other.

I

Differences between parents and their children's mates may arise over what seem to be trifles. But these trifles may spoil a relationship needlessly, as is evident from the following:

LETTER: *My daughter is married for the past four years to a highly intelligent, well-educated and personable young man of whom my husband and I are extremely fond. In all this time, he has never addressed either of us by name or title.*

When he wants to talk to us, he manages to attract our attention. We find this a great source of annoyance. Despite the fact that we have spoken to him on innumerable occasions, telling him just how we feel about this, he still finds it difficult to address us by our title, mother- and fa-

ther-in-law. We would be perfectly satisfied to be called by our first names, but he has done nothing.

How can we adjust to this situation? As explained above, we like him very much and we would not want this to cause a rift. Yet my husband and I are very unhappy about all this. We would appreciate any light you can shed on this painful subject.

ANSWER: Most frequently, bringing a painful subject out into the open and discussing it does relieve the tension and the hurt. Sometimes, however, a direct approach like this can create a problem or delay an adjustment which would have taken place sooner, had it not been built up into a major crisis.

When a person is self-conscious about his relationships in a new situation, it does not help him become more at ease to be told that this attitude or behavior is making other people unhappy. This only increases his self-consciousness. He may then feel hostile to the people who, instead of considering what a hard time he is having, are only concerned about what they want, and how not getting it affects them.

A young husband's hesitation or indecision about how to address his wife's parents is not an unusual occurrence. Most of the time, when it is left to the young couple themselves, and the in-laws do not allow themselves to get too impatient or annoyed about it, some nomenclature for addressing the in-laws is arrived at.

Often it is the young person's attitude and feelings about his own parents that determine how he will address himself to his wife's parents. A person who has felt hostile to his own father may find it difficult to address anyone else by that name. The converse can also take place. A person who has felt too lovingly dependent on his parents, and therefore guilty about leaving them for marriage, may find it almost impossible to call anyone else Mom and Dad. This would be to take away from his parents something that belongs exclusively to them.

Naturally, the attitudes and behavior of the parents-in-law can effect the new in-law's reaction to them. If they are too possessive of their daughter and continue to treat her like their little girl, who just happens to be rooming with someone else, then the son-in-law will certainly not want to play into this objectionable pattern. Calling them by the parental titles which they covet could possibly give them a feeling of power over him, as if there were some hidden magic in the words Father and Mother. To a young man who wants to be treated as the head of his household and is still sensitive about it, any communication that would seem to diminish respect for his position would be unacceptable.

Far fewer daughters-in-law hesitate to address their in-laws directly. The female, whose dependence on others is an accepted part of her femininity, does not feel that she is giving up any of her independence or individuality in acquiring two additional parents. Interestingly, the in-laws that are usually most complained about are the females— the daughter-in-law and the mother-in-law. But pretty words and appropriate titles are not always the key to peace and contentment.

The "innumerable" occasions that you have talked to your son-in-law about your annoyance seem to have lengthened the time before he can, of his own free will, address you directly and by a name of his choice. Although you say you do not want to cause a rift because of this, you must surely realize that it has become a point of dissension, perhaps even of rifts among you all. Probably you have no ally in your daughter on this issue. The young couple may feel, perhaps rightfully, that you are attaching undue importance to words and titles. They expect, perhaps, a little more understanding of the young man's shyness, if that is what it is.

If this is the only fault you can find with this highly educated, intelligent and personable young man, then your daughter and you, her parents, are fortunate indeed. When he treats your precious daughter lovingly and kindly, he is being loving to you in deeds, instead of only in words.

Since you were so open about your criticism of him on "innumerable" occasions, you must have a pretty open and direct relationship with him. You might now tell your son-in-law that perhaps you have made an undue fuss about this matter, that it really doesn't matter so much to you, and that, as far as you are concerned, henceforth, the subject is dropped.

Quite often such a situation is resolved when the young couple have children. It is easier for them to address the in-laws as Grandpa and Grandma. In a way, this is a more realistic appellation. Somehow, Mother-in-law and Father-in-law have never become a common form of address. For some people, calling their in-laws by their first names seems a sign of disrespect. When you become grandparents to his children, your son-in-law may be emotionally able to accept you more readily as parents.

II

Things may not always be as they seem. Parents who disapprove of their child's choice of a mate, like the parents in the following letter, may leap to the wrong conclusions, using what are really very flimsy reasons to excuse what is really inexcusable conduct.

LETTER: *My son, a college man with several degrees and holding an executive position, is married to a college girl, the same age as he is. Despite the fact that they have two children, their marriage is not a happy one.*

Prior to their marriage, the girl requested that we write a large amount of life insurance in his name, making her the beneficiary, of course. Needless to say her request was not complied with. She had told us that she wanted to protect herself.

Recently, my daughter-in-law was making a business transaction. When she and I were alone, I had pointed out to her very tactfully how she could save $100 on the deal. Her reply was: "Money does not mean that much to me. I will make your son work harder because he has to live with me." I rarely visit with them or give advice.

My daughter, younger and married, as well as my unmarried son, insist that I tell their brother about his wife's latest declaration of her feelings for him, otherwise they will.

I am in a quandary. Perhaps it is important to mention that their courtship was of short duration.

ANSWER: Perhaps it is important to recall that although their courtship was of short duration, their marriage has endured. Observers who attempt to make judgments about the relationships of others should be aware of their own psychological motivations which are inherent in the task they undertake. When the observers are insiders, members of a family group, their own wishes and problems sometimes distort their judgment.

Thus, parents who do not like the in-laws their children bring into the family may interpret their actions or words to mean that the couple dislike each other and are not very happy in their union. Often these hostile attitudes or remarks are really meant for the parents of the in-law. That they prefer to see it as an assault on their child, rather than on themselves is quite natural, though erroneous.

In criticizing your daughter-in-law you are really being critical of your son for having made such a poor choice of a wife. With all his fine educational achievements and all his vocational success, he is not very bright to have chosen a person who is out to fleece him.

Perhaps you had hoped that, once he, your first-born, finished his education and began to achieve success at work, you would reap some rewards. But suddenly, he not only found a girl, but did so in a hurry, and left all of you for her. To you, this probably was both startling and shocking, and you may have shown your disapproval of the girl without necessarily being aware of it.

What you said and what you asked at the time may have given her clues to your feelings, namely, that you wished you could break up the relationship. It may have been in response to this implicit attack that, to protect herself, the young wife-to-be made her requests, brash though they may have sounded. To stop undue demands on her husband-to-be by his family, she made some demands of her own. When these were denied by his family, she could then feel free to reject their demands on him.

The stingy one constantly hoards and finds satisfaction in the growing pile; the grasping one constantly calls on others to give to her and feed her so that she may be satisfied. Even while accusing your daughter-in-law of being very grasping, you belittle her ability to make money deals, and credit yourself with being much wiser, more able than she. The feeling you may give her is that she is not very bright or acute in money matters.

It would seem that with a family of children and grandchildren to occupy your time and attention, you should have more positive things to do than fostering dissension between your son and his wife. It is certainly no service to anyone to get his sister and brother involved. Their insistence that you tell the older brother about his wife's latest declaration may be motivated by a bit of envy on their part because of the favoritism which you have always expressed for your first-born. They hide behind the legitimate cloak of agreeing with their mother, to express their jealousy.

Whatever the outcome of your son's marriage, you should certainly remove yourself from the contest. The role of the watchful mother who protects her youngster from the females around him is not appropriate now.

You should want, above all else, for the marriage to continue and prosper, and you should do everything in your power not to interfere. Eliminating your "helpful" alerting of the rest of the family would be a step in the right direction. You must accept the devotion of your son to the female of his choice, and his dedication to making the marriage work.

Interest yourself in worthwhile causes. You may then feel more worthwhile as a mother, without the need to judge and supervise your grown children.

III

Outright hostility between in-laws usually results from injuries done by both parties to each other. The mother who brings up the problem in this letter, and the daughter-in-law involved, both had a certain amount of right and a certain amount of wrong on their sides.

LETTER: *My oldest son, now twenty-four, married a girl who had been married before. She became pregnant before this first marriage, but my son married her and raised her little girl as his very own child. They have one child of their own.*

Of course, this was hard on me at first. But I have since done everything in my power to help. Still, she doesn't seem to want to accept me.

On my last visit (they live in another state, 400 miles away), I brought toys and clothes for the children and some things for my son and daughter-in-law. She turned to me and asked if I was trying to buy her love. I was so upset, I could not answer.

I love my grandchildren, but I don't think I should be insulted each time I go there.

ANSWER: In-law problems often start long before a marriage takes place.

When minor differences, like those over plans for the wedding, are blown up and given even greater importance than they deserve, it tells a story of non-acceptance and hostility toward the in-law which cannot be expressed openly. After the wedding, these dissensions continue, and the acts of the in-law chosen as the reason for the attack often continue to be as superficial and unimportant as they were at the beginning.

Sometimes, parents are justified in their anxious concern about the girl their son has chosen to marry. They naturally hold back when they learn that this girl has had problems in her past and they wonder whether these will repeat themselves in one form or another after the couple are married.

But one mistake or one emotional upset should not stigmatize a person for life. Some people do falter and fall. But then they pick themselves up and begin to operate in a mature way.

It was all to the good, of course, that your daughter-in-law was able to tell your son about her past. It indicates a degree of emotional health and security, and perhaps most important, it shows that she does not continue to hold it against herself.

If the facts about her previous marriage became known to you through prying behind their backs, it may have something to do with your daughter-in-law's attitude toward you. However, if the young couple told you this on their own, then your rejection of her which followed must have been a great hurt to her. She had been honest and direct with you, but you didn't respond as she had hoped you would. This could have made her feel that you would always hold this past episode in her life against her.

Once a loving mother sees her son deriving happiness and fulfillment from his marriage, she usually expresses acceptance and even gratitude to the wife who has helped him achieve this. But the response is not so quick from the young wife who was once rejected. She will be suspicious of any friendly overtures and hesitant to accept them, for fear that they are only a cover-up for hostility that still exists underneath.

It was certainly not the most gracious way of responding to your generosity and thoughtfulness for your daughter-in-law to ask if you were trying to buy her affection. However, she may have been saying by this that she still feels rejected, and that before she can accept you fully, you must show that you sincerely accept her.

She may be right that you are to some extent over-giving, to make up for what you withheld in the past. However, if she feels free enough to make such a remark, you should feel free enough to tell her that you do love the entire family and are grateful for the happiness they have brought to each other and to you.

The gifts that you bring will then become symbols

of the love and understanding which you are now prepared to give them. If she takes a little longer to accept their emotional worth, instead of their financial worth, you should be patient and tolerant. In the end, you will all be beneficiaries.

IV

Occasionally a son- or daughter-in-law is discovered to suffer from a serious psychological problem, after the couple have been married for a number of years. The mother who wrote the following letter was faced with just such a problem. The question that troubled her which also troubles many others in similar situations, is, how does one handle such a delicate situation, without hurting one's own child too much?

LETTER: *My daughter, twenty-four, married out of her faith six years ago. We didn't like him at the beginning, but learned to accept him and have been on good terms since.*

The past few years, we have noticed money missing, but said nothing, since we couldn't prove anything. Once he offered to go and have a prescription filled. When he returned, he claimed he lost two dollars.

Two weeks ago I caught him going to my bag. When he heard me coming, he left hastily. My wallet and dollar bills were lying around. I haven't spoken to him since. I cannot bear to look at him. I am keeping quiet because of my daughter and her two children, five and two.

My husband feels I should forget it and start talking to him again. I feel if I do, he'll resort to the same thing.

My daughter told me he is upset because I am angry with him. I'm sure she doesn't know her husband is a thief.

The very day he went to my pocketbook, my husband had given my daughter a check for one hundred fifty dollars for their vacation.

ANSWER: Sometimes people look for a flaw in an individual's behavior to rationalize their hostility and lack of acceptance of him. They may, in this quest, see in the person's words or actions meanings that aren't actually there.

In prying and probing to find something unacceptable in the other, the person psychologically wards off inquiry about herself, where others might possibly discover things about her which she herself doesn't like.

The way in which you are handling this situation suggests that your basic displeasure is with your daughter, rather than with your son-in-law. You may have gone along with her marriage because you had no other alternative, and felt she was doing her parents a great disservice by putting them in such a position. Marrying out of her faith was the first assault. That she chose someone you felt was her inferior was then seen as a reflection on the job you did as a mother.

If your son-in-law really has kleptomaniacal tendencies, and what you saw was a fact, then neither silence nor resuming communication with him and acting as if it never took place, will solve the problem.

Silence is a form of disapproval which only serves to justify the misbehavior and is certainly no way to communicate the right message. To start talking to him again, as if nothing had happened, is also no solution. Perhaps you are avoiding a face-to-face confrontation because you yourself have some doubts about your conclusions.

If you are absolutely sure that you are right, then you should give him the benefit of correction. It might be best for your husband to handle this matter and discuss with your son-in-law what he did. He should not be accusatory or judgmental, but should tell the young man that this is a psychological problem which, fortunately, does respond to therapy. After a man-to-man talk, it should be left to your son-in-law as to how and when he wants to take this matter up with his wife.

If money for therapy is a problem, he could contact the family agency of his religious persuasion for help, or for a referral to a guidance clinic. This would communicate to him that his in-laws really care and want to help.

Until he goes for help, and hopefully he will, you and your husband should be careful not to leave wallets or purses lying around. This constitutes a silent invitation to disobey, and practically seduces the person to misbehave.

V

Newlyweds have not just one set of parents to deal with that can create difficulties, but two sets, and it is not only the relations of each set with the newlyweds, but of each set with each other. The double in-law problem which this letter reveals, is further complicated by an obviously delicate marital situation between one set of parents who are actually competing with their own grown children.

LETTER: *My older son has been married one year. We are delighted with our new daughter. Having two sons, we never realized how lovely daughters can be.*

Last year we were all together on Mother's Day and had dinner at a restaurant. This year we were left out. Her parents had them for dinner and excluded us.

My daughter-in-law and I were very close. She told

me how lucky she was to have me for a mother-in-law. I told them how hurt I was. I believe in being honest.

Our daughter-in law's parents are much younger, very well-to-do, of the "jet-set" and lead a very gay life. Her parents separated about ten months ago. They reconciled last month, and are again living together.

I must add that by the time my son and his wife came over on Mother's Day, we had gone to my sister's. They left a gift and a card. My daughter-in-law has since explained that this was the way her mother wanted it, and she was put on the spot. She hopes I can understand and forgive her. I have.

ANSWER: Actually, a young person's relationship with her own parents determines to a large extent the kind of relationship she will have with her in laws.

Sometimes, a good relationship between mother-in-law and daughter-in-law fulfills some need growing out of the earlier years. If her mother was a competitor who had always paid more attention to her own needs than to her daughter's she will dream of a mother-in-law who will be the kind of mother she never had.

The mother-in-law at first is very grateful to have a daughter-in-law who looks upon her as a mother. But in time, she will inevitably expect the daughter-in-law to give her the special attention, love and regard shown a real mother. When this is not forthcoming, she sees it as ungracious and ungrateful conduct.

It is very confusing to growing children when parents act younger than their years, especially when they lead the so-called gay life of the "jet-set." It says that the parents don't want to grow up, and that they are acting more like peers than parents.

The tensions that led to the temporary separation

must have gone on for quite a while. As many children do, this daughter may have felt somewhat responsible for the alienation.

While the in-laws were adjusting to the reconciliation, they may have felt that being with others on a parents' day might be somewhat embarrassing. Also, they wanted to be with their side of the family, and show their children that they were back together and would hopefully stay that way.

It is hard to understand why arrangements were not made for your son and his wife to spend some of Mother's Day with your side of the family. Perhaps your son was embarrassed about bringing up the subject because he knew how badly his wife felt about it. For him to have told you the news, may have meant talking against his in-laws and could have been seen as an act of disloyalty to his wife.

That you and your daughter-in-law could express your hurts and regrets to each other shows a fine relationship. To avoid hurts in the future, you should ask ahead of time about their plans and when it would be most convenient for you to celebrate happy times together.

PART II

Between Husband and Wife

✍ 5. LOVE GROWS OLDER–AND COLDER?

Forty or fifty years ago, it was considered odd and even abnormal if married couples in their middle years engaged in sex as frequently as they had when they were younger, and outrageous if they admitted it or were proud of the fact. Today this attitude is considered old-fashioned. Sex, for Middle Generation couples can be, indeed should be just as enjoyable, loving and satisfying an experience as it was at any previous time in their married lives. Love need not grow colder, as it grows older.

Methods and circumstances of gratification and foreplay may change along with frequency as the couple grows older. But these changes only indicate that the couple is still young and flexible. Some couples like to stay with the old and usual. Others become bored, unstimulated and unstimulating and prefer to experiment with something new, becoming perennially involved and stimulated, each to their own tastes, and equally happy with their results.

Sometimes a Middle Generation husband and wife become frightened when their sexual desires are not aroused as frequently as in the beginning, or when the experience turns out not to be as satisfying as usual. Actually, such fluctuations go on all through married life. If they were to look back in reassessment, they would be reassured and not frightened.

When they were younger and experienced any ebbing in their sexual feelings for each other, they soon discovered that the condition was only temporary, and that their normal sexual pattern soon re-established itself. In their middle years, however, they may worry that the passing years have made them less desirable, each to the other, and that their waning strength and vigor, evident in so many other areas, will leave them less potent sexually.

The frequency of sexual activity in the lives of any married couple, at any age, has its highs and lows. Naturally, times of stress and strain within and outside the family affect the couple's sex life. For some, sex affords a safe harbor from the storms of life. For others, sex and turmoil are incompatible, and they must wait for the calm to settle again.

Complete love is made up of two components, romantic and tender love. Both must always be present. There is no doubt that with aging, certain physiological changes take place that affect sexual activity to some degree. At that point, tender love is more predominant, but romantic love is still there. This is now expressed in the mindfulness and consideration that each shows for the other. Thus, neither husband nor wife feels that the vigorous life is slipping away from them, even though they may no longer be able to operate sexually on the same level of former years.

I

No matter how compatible a couple may have been sexually all through their married life together, it is always a surprise and a shock when sexual problems arise to disturb the tranquility of their middle years.

Quite suddenly, one or the other may feel unable or unwilling to participate. The cause may be a temporary physiological disfunction related to illness, as in the case described in the letter which follows, or it may be psychological. Behind the latter may be some old fear related to sex which suddenly rears its head, or some long-suppressed sense of guilt, perhaps from indulging in sex too frequently, or in some imagined forbidden manner. The sudden recurrence of these old fears may bring on an attack of what can perhaps be described as a kind of sexual "stage-fright." Terrified that he will not be able to perform as well as expected, or afraid that she will forget her lines, the husband or the wife may freeze up and withdraw, immobilized.

For some women this happens when they anticipate their change of life far in advance, and mistakenly "prepare" themselves for the time when they believe that they will have less and less desire, and even have to withdraw from their sex life altogether. The man can go through a very similar emotional experience. Sometimes he identifies with his wife and anticipates a kind of male menopause, wherein he is not too sure anymore that he is all man. By not engaging in sex at all, he will avoid revealing his doubts and deficiencies about his sexuality. This transient impotency, for that is all it usually is, calls for patience and forebearance on the part of the other partner. In a relatively short time it may pass, and normalcy will be restored to both partners, with a better relationship resulting from having weathered the storm.

LETTER: *We are married almost eighteen years and have two children. My husband is forty-eight and I am thirty-seven. About two and a half months ago my husband suffered a bleeding ulcer attack which hospitalized him for almost two weeks. He is still under a doctor's care and on a diet.*

Ever since he suffered the attack, we have had no sex life. He claims to have desire mentally, but to be physically incapable. I love my husband, and this situation has made a nervous wreck of me.

I imagine he no longer loves or desires me. He feels utterly hopeless and that he has lost his virility forever. He says he would even give me a divorce, which I don't want.

I am so miserable. My doctor recommends that I leave him alone sexually until he comes to me.

ANSWER: Without underestimating for a moment the great contribution of a full and satisfied sex life to a continuing happy marriage, the memory of past satisfactions of eighteen years of happy and loving relationship with your husband should help tide you over this trying time now.

As you must surely know, there is no physical connection between your husband's ulcer attack and his present inability to consummate the sex act. Nor does this by any means denote that he has lost his virility. The impotence which he is experiencing is most likely a passing phase and a result of the emotional impact which the ulcer attack had on him.

All people react to an operation on their bodies with feelings of lessened worth. But most people get over it rather quickly when they resume their normal life and get back into the flow of their usual activities again.

Internal bleeding is in some ways a more assaultive blow to a person's ego than an operation. It can't be seen, it comes and goes as it wishes and is felt to be uncontrollable, unless the body is cut into. Besides, there is always the accompanying fear, even after the operation, that the bleeding might begin again without warning, as it did before.

To a man, bleeding that comes and goes almost at its own will may be associated unconsciously with women and their menstrual flow. For a man, therefore, such bleeding may mean a flowing away of part of his manliness.

Like a man who has had a heart attack or who suffers from high blood pressure, the one who has bled fears that any exertion—especially for pleasure—will tax his remaining strength and cause another attack. He immobilizes his desires, just as he limits his activities or diet. Unconsciously, he makes himself impotent as a means of self-protection, even though it involves self-denial.

During this period of psychological recovery along with physical recovery, the individual may see in the desire of another for him a selfish demand, utterly lacking in thoughtfulness or consideration for him.

The doctor's suggestion that you wait for your husband to make the advances to you is a good one. It makes the man feel less manly for the woman to make the loving overtures and take the initiative in what is usually a man's prerogative.

But this certainly does not mean that you should leave your husband alone or in any way make him feel that he is less loved, or that he will be ostracized and left out until he is able to resume his loving sexual activities as a husband.

II

Sometimes, what begins as a temporary break in the couple's normal sexual routine leads to a permanent break, and to an interruption in communications as well. Suddenly the old pattern appears to be shattered, and they cannot seem to put it back together again. When the causes behind such a rupture are deep-seated, they need exploring and clarification if the relationship is to be re-established and to continue. The couple in this letter found a relatively small circumstance to trigger the annoyance or hostility that had been there for quite some time.

LETTER: *We were two people who fell head over heels in love at practically our first meeting. We married. This was his second and my first. Six years ago, after twelve glorious happy years, my husband stopped being intimate with me. I was sick for a few months previous to his stopping and we started to sleep in separate beds for my comfort. It was my suggestion at first, then he kept it up.*

To me there is much more to a marriage than sex, so it didn't bother me, although at times I'll admit I would have enjoyed some. I couldn't bring myself to say anything about this issue. He continued to be very kind to me as always. We went on a long trip and, much to my surprise, he asked for twin beds.

My husband is thirteen years my senior. He is fifty-eight years old. He must have felt guilty, for he explained without my saying a word that he was getting too old. I accepted this and because I loved him, it didn't matter to me.

Recently we moved to another state where his father runs a business. He took charge of the office for his father and in no time at all I learned that he was stepping out with his private secretary. What can one think, except that he is having relations with her? She is a divorcée of many years. He doesn't think I know this.

What shall I do? I'm still very much in love with him.

ANSWER: While sex alone cannot make a marriage, the denial of it by one partner to another can help break it up. There are more emotionally broken marriages than is generally recognized where the couple still stay together.

This does not include the couples who, in the first

place, wanted only a companion, friend, or a helper, in a mate. They never desired physical closeness because it might challenge their faulty concept of masculinity or femininity. Such a husband feels he is a man because he goes out to work and supports the house. The wife feels she is a female because she cooks, cleans and looks after her man. Such couples are often childless. When their sporadic sexual activity does not result in the conception of a child, they give it up.

The attitude of such people toward sex is often that it is something bad. It must not be used to bring enjoyment for the sake of enjoyment alone. It is permissible only for the conception of a child, i.e., for procreation, but not for recreation.

This is a distortion of the facts of life and love, and it can rob people of almost every other pleasure.

When there is a wide difference in age between the husband and the wife, she sees a great deal of her father in him, and he may see a great deal of a daughter in her. After the first excitement of the honeymoon, sex fades in importance, and they enjoy a loving but not a very physical relationship. Interestingly, while such couples would strongly assert that they miss the physical closeness, they really do not want it. They may have occasional sexual experiences on the outside, and when caught, do not want a divorce, but want to be forgiven. They promise never to stray again, but may repeat their extramarital wanderings, hoping that the mate will again forgive them. The excitement of the angry episodes of discovery, punishment and forgiveness re-evokes and replaces the excitement of the lovemaking of the earlier romantic years.

You not only started the sexual separation, but you continued it after you became well again, to suit your own comfort and convenience. You may have been waiting with some apprehension for him to make the first move to get together again, and when he didn't, you found being left alone more pleasurable than being approached sexually.

When you did not invite your husband to return to your bed, he felt it as a rejection. He may still feel young and virile at fifty-eight, but you made him feel undesirable and older than his years. In ascribing guilt to him for abiding by your own wish not to have sexual relations, you are really shirking the responsibility for both the past and the present situation.

This method of blaming him for your own acts may again be in operation in your accusations of infidelity against your husband with regard to his supposed stepping out with the private secretary. If this is mere speculation based on flimsy, unsupported evidence, then you ought to discard it. Unjustified accusations can lead a person to do what he is accused of, in order to retaliate and to hurt the accuser.

Both of you are young enough to enjoy the expression of your love through sexual relations. Sometimes a person may feel it is easier to start from scratch than to patch up what has gone wrong. This is a mistake.

Marriage counseling could clear up why you moved away from your husband, and why he was willing to go along with the separation. With the roadblocks out of the way, you might re-establish a good and mutually fulfilling sex life, perhaps a better and deeper one than what you have previously experienced.

III

Sexual incompatibility may assume many forms. It is usually rooted in some facet of the marriage relationship which finds negative expression in sexual terms. The entire marriage relationship then falls apart over this issue. It may be triggered by quibbles over dominance between the partners, or the definition of their separate roles within the family structure; it may involve the relationship between parents and children, or a host of other factors.

Whatever the issue, the entire family is sure to be affected in some way. Where dependent children are involved, their normal pattern of emotional and sexual development can be disrupted. This is particularly true if the children are adolescents. The sexual self-identification of young boys and girls may become confused, and their emotional growth stunted, if the family differences between the parents are fought out on the sexual battleground. As the letter below illustrates, such battles tend to spread, and sweep friends as well as family into the contest. This can be a subtle form of "sex en masse."

LETTER: *My husband is sexually very prudish. My boy, who is fifteen, is aware of this, and when he wants something of a sexual nature explained, he asks me into his room and confides his problems to me. I, being broadminded, explain things to him in a straightforward manner.*

Also, when our family circle gathers, and an off-color joke is told, my husband either walks away or tells me later that he doesn't go for such things, and that sex is something he can take or leave. He is perfectly contented to spend his evenings reading newspapers until 1 A.M. every night.

I am a romantic and attractive woman in my forties. It doesn't seem to enter his mind that I go to bed every night frustrated. Yet, if any member of my family should mention all the boyfriends I had before my marriage, he boils with jealousy, or if I should admire a TV actor or male movie star, he also gets that jealous look.

He loves me in a platonic way, but I am a woman

with strong and sensitive feelings. His actions toward me are an insult to my womanhood. If I mention divorce, he acts hysterical. He isn't impotent physically.

What can I do?

ANSWER: It is not only withholding that can be frustrating. Teasing, that takes the initiative away from the male, can also be devastating.

Where two people are involved, each one may both offend and complain about being offended, in his own individual way. The wife may say that her mate is not appreciative enough of her as a female, and she is not getting enough sex, as a result. The husband may say that her demands, made directly and indirectly, even in public, belittle and castrate him as a male, and therefore he punishes her by not giving in.

Exhibitionism is a form of aggression and can be expressed verbally as well as in action. Telling off-color stories is a way of making sexual overtures in words. For some, this kind of stimulation is satisfying in and of itself, and needs no follow-ups. Others are stimulated sufficiently to want to follow it up soon after by some kind of sexual activity. A person's mate may, however, find it repugnant to be approached on this basis.

Telling off-color stories in front of children is not only exhibitionistic, but harmful to the children. While very often missing the point of the story completely, the implications they draw about the grown-ups' self-revealed weaknesses are not good for them or the grown-ups. Instead of being the highest expression of love, it becomes something dirty, a suitable subject for "dirty" jokes.

When the adults around them engage in this kind of verbal sex-play, children often become apprehensive and tense about their own newborn sexual feelings. If the grown-ups to whom they should be able to turn for guidance are unable to control their own feelings, how can the children ever hope to succeed in doing so.

Your husband may appear prudish because he takes his position at the other extreme. He may really be reacting not so much to the telling of off-color stories in public, as to your discussions of sex with your son in private.

A boy naturally turns to his father for edification about sexual matters. Sometimes a mother who cannot let a good relationship develop between father and son, extends an open invitation to the boy to come and discuss such matters with her. This makes the father appear like a prude. Talks about sex with the opposite-sex parent become more a matter of sex stimulation than of sex education.

Some wives want sex more as proof of their desirability than for the satisfaction of a genuine sexual need. Husbands sense this, and feel that they are being misused. Wives, on the other hand, sense it when they are used only for physical release, instead of out of mutual love.

The person who is really being used in your battle with your husband is your fifteen-year-old son. It makes your husband and your son feel excluded from each other's life, which prevents the establishment of the normal father-son relationship that every youngster needs.

Your family has evidently been made aware of your reaction to your husband's attitudes about sex, and they join in the teasing which he finds so offensive. Neither is it cricket to use the boyfriends of yesteryear or the threat of a divorce to arouse and excite him. Being mocked is not a healthy stimulant to love and desire. A person who lives under a constant challenge or a threat of punishment cannot function at his best.

From now on, his father should answer your son's questions about sex. You should respect your husband's wishes about the kind of talk he deems permissible in his presence. A child's sexual questions cannot all be answered at this age, nor can all his wishes be gratified. A "dirty" joke may arouse him, only to leave him frustrated. There is no point in making this his daily lot in life.

To enjoy the kind of sex life you want, you must treat your husband as a desirable person, and not merely as a tool to satisfy your desires. A woman may certainly tell her husband how desirable and lovable she finds him as a male. This does not violate the concept of femininity. To such an approach your husband would respond enthusiastically, and he would then begin to seek you out on his own initiative.

A boy of fifteen best learns about sex in depth from the relationship between his parents, rather than from books or sex talks. A loving and respectful relationship between the parents answers the youngster's basic questions, which have more to do with feelings than with facts.

IV

Communication between marriage partners is of prime importance at all times. Even after many years of marriage, when the couple are in their middle years, the need for such communication between husband and wife is as crucial as ever.

We are concerned about the communication gap between the generations. But this does not break up families, as does the communication gap between a husband and wife. Sometimes when the lines of communication are ruptured, either the husband or the wife may try to re-open them in a somewhat unorthodox manner, by recruiting third parties to act as involuntary "hot lines."

The messages that start coming through are generally loud

and clear, but they may not be deciphered in the same way by the husband, at one end of the line, and by the wife, at the other. Sex may be what causes the "static" in the circuit, as in the following case.

LETTER: *My husband, at fifty-five, still maintains an extremely healthy sex drive. In conversation with other people he will usually manage to get the subject around to sex. He has, on several occasions, asked of people with whom he feels he can take the liberty, such questions as "How's your sex life?" or "How often do you have sex relations?"*

One of these people has complained to me of this habit and would like to understand it. So would I. Is it because he is so highly sexed, or because he finds his own sex life not gratifying enough, and is disappointed in himself as a sex partner?

I do not require sex as often as he, and am a rather passive partner.

ANSWER: A frequently heard complaint from couples who, with the years, have developed difficulties in communication is that they get up-to-date news of what their mate is thinking or doing only when they are in the company of friends and listen in on the mate's conversation.

One reason is that the company of friends can be used as a platform for the discussion of a subject which one of the pair feels might develop into a fight, if brought up in private. Before others, the discussion becomes a generalized intellectual exercise, and is safe. In addition, the listening audience participates in the discussion, acting as both mediator and monitor.

Such public discussion of a private problem is a form of exhibitionism, which carries with it a certain amount of gratification. Gratification can also be obtained from prying and probing into the intimate lives of others. People who cannot obtain satisfaction from doing, often try to substitute gratification from viewing. A person who is sexually frustrated in his marital life may use this approach to ease his tensions.

If you, as his wife, make your husband feel that he is an oddity because he continues to desire sex, he will be driven to seek evidence to the contrary in public and in your presence. You cannot then question his veracity. That your husband is still so virile and desirous of you is a tribute both to his emotional and physical youthfulness, and to your desirability and attractiveness as a female.

It is easier to accuse another of wanting too much, than to accuse oneself of not wanting any, or not wanting to give enough. You seem almost to welcome the complaints of friends, which you use to justify your passivity and to accuse your husband of overactivity.

A couple who love each other recognize that timing, frequency, and modes of expression are unique. They then try to harmonize with each other's rhythms, modifying their own sexual wishes and behavior accordingly.

Your husband will stop questioning others when your responses do not make him question himself and his normality. It is you who are making yourself old before your time, by giving up a more active sexual life for one of withdrawal.

V

There is a current trend toward "uni-sex" in fashions, where boys and girls, and even some husbands and wives, tend to dress alike in some respects. In the Scandinavian countries, some husbands and wives have even taken to switching their marital roles—she goes out to work, while he stays home and takes care of the family.

This blurring of gender distinctions in the general population may only be a passing fad, but on a deeper level, it is rooted in certain latent bisexual tendencies which are found in a certain small proportion of men and women.

The sexual roles of a husband and wife are usually clearly defined, and given the normal physical and emotional equipment, there are fairly well-fixed mutual limits to what is possible, desirable and healthy. If, however, one or the other of the partners suddenly begins to desire a far-out variation, it is a startling development to the spouse. When it requires, in effect, a switch in roles, or the assumption of some part of the partner's role, then a new manifestation of an old deep-seated problem has entered into the marriage relationship. This is not solved by being accepted by the partner, as this couple found.

LETTER: *My husband holds an important and responsible position. There has been an unusual amount of pressure lately, both at work, and, due to some family problems related to his mother, at home.*

During the last three or four months he suddenly began to wear feminine undergarments before making love, like black stockings, and high-heeled shoes. His virility and ardor towards me have not diminished. While I am not revolted by all this, I am not stimulated, either.

Lately, he even wears panties to the office, and I discovered that he wore long silk stockings to a black-tie dinner the other night. Besides the possibility of the embarrassment of discovery and subsequent scandal, I am worried about just what this means. He claims that this is his form of relaxation. He has no homosexual desires and certainly is in every other respect a normal man.

I am really worried about his health. He is only forty-seven-years-old, and generally a rather balanced person. He plays golf and bridge, and normally that was relaxation enough.

ANSWER: Transvestitism usually shows itself much earlier than in your husband's case.

In the history of the transvestite there is usually a very permissive mother who gives in to the boy's wishes, and makes jewelry, lipsticks, dresses and other apparel easily available to him. By allowing this kind of play to go on, she gives her overt and tacit approval to his peculiar fantasies and play-acting. Most often it is kept as a secret between mother and son.

Certain types of homosexuals may like to dress up in female clothing. However, transvestites are not necessarily homosexuals. Wearing female clothing is, in the early years, a way of getting close to the mother. By putting on her clothes, the little boy gains a kind of quasi-physical contact with her, which plays into his fantasies, but is far less guilt-provoking than any overt sexual fantasies.

Later on, it becomes part of the foreplay in marriage, and provides stimulation for the gratification to come.

Often, in the history of the transvestite, there is not only a rather doting and dominating mother, but also great disappointment on her part about the sex of her child. By dressing up like a little girl, he satisfies his mother's wish.

When such a man marries, he often chooses a wife who is just as authoritative a personality as his mother was. He feels protected by her authority and also wants her to take the initiative in their sex life. When, after marriage, the transvestitism reveals itself, the wife is usually not too shocked or even too greatly surprised. Like the mother of the trans-vestite, she gives in most of the time and permits him to engage in his transvestite behavior, as long as it is kept within the confines of their private life. When there is any danger of its being discovered on the outside, the wife begins to agitate and show concern.

The danger in this practice lies in that it may gradually lose some of its excitement when it is done only in private. Then, as you have observed, the urge to add a fillip to it may drive the person to seek a larger audience. Your husband knows that to be discovered will hurt his reputation and his job.

Psychiatric help is really necessary in such cases, and it often can be very helpful. Let your husband know that in making this suggestion you are motivated not by criticism, but by love for him.

Once he overcomes the need to use these deviate means to gain satisfaction, he will be able to fulfill himself in a more meaningful way, both in his love relationship and in his work.

✍ 6. SECOND HONEYMOON —OR IS IT?

By the time they have reached their middle years, most married couples have weathered the usual stresses of their earlier years, when two different personalities were adjusting to each other, careers were being built and families established. Surely, by this time, with the children either grown and on their own, or very near it, the Middle Generation couple has the right to expect calm lagoons and safe harbors.

Yet these middle years can be very difficult ones for them, despite the outward appearance of a settled and happy marriage. How surprised their friends are when they discover that the married couple whose happiness they have always taken for granted is visiting a marriage counselor, or is separated and on the verge of a divorce! How did it happen, they want to know. What could possibly come between two people who have lived together for so many years?

What happens is not too difficult to understand once one gets a look at the "inside story." With the children grown to maturity, a good deal of the load of the responsibility has been lifted from the marriage. There are no longer others to be concerned with, certainly not to the same degree. Now there are only "he and she," just as there were when they began their married career together. But what a different couple they are, after fifteen, twenty or thirty years of living together behind them.

They are no longer the young, eager lovers of their early or mid-twenties with a lifetime ahead of them. These two people are now, once again, face to face with each other, and also face to face with the full realization of the changes that time has wrought.

While it is true that they have changed gradually and together, nevertheless their only major concerns now have to do with themselves and each other. Now the old dreams and expectations are revived and are compared with the reality of what has actually happened. At this time, too, all the annoyances, frustrations and disagreements that had to take a back seat while the children were growing and the parents working so hard, now are brought out. These grievances, some of them petty, seem to have grown greater over the years, because they were repressed. Now, any trivial episode can trigger an outburst which is usually out of proportion to the act or word that caused it.

And what a squall it can be! It could be a case of who forgets to put the top back on the toothpaste tube. But quite often the basic differences involved are serious, having to do with deep-seated personality problems, financial difficulties of long standing, the tug-of-war of dominance between the partners, not to mention sexual problems. One hears of enough Middle Generation marriages that are in trouble to indicate that this is no trivial or occasional phenomenon.

It will be interesting to examine the how, the why and the wherefore of this fascinating phenomenon.

I

It is surprising that two people can live together and never really talk to each other. Naturally, there has to be some communication. No family can exist without it. No two people can produce children, feed and clothe them and bring them up without, in some measure, communicating.

And yet, it seems, it is possible for a married couple to live together for decades, maintaining a blanket of silence about some of the things that really matter the most to both of them. They never say the words or express the thoughts to each other that might open the door to understanding.

When such a situation comes to light in a marriage of many years standing, the most natural question is, who isn't talking to whom? But the really important question is, who isn't listening?

LETTER: *I have been married for nearly twenty years to a wonderful man. However, our relationship, I always felt, is superficial. I feel I can't confide in or even talk to him like a friend. Emotionally, he is enclosed in a tight shell. His attitude is: "That's your opinion."*

Making a good living is the essence of his life. Psychiatry and family counseling are unspeakable words. When I try to relate how I feel about something, he winds up with terribly hurt feelings. He feels I am picking on him.

We have three wonderful daughters, aged sixteen, fourteen and eight. He is a marvelous father and adores them. Perhaps because I had such a marvelous relationship with my father, I am expecting too much from my husband. He is a college graduate, and up-to-date intellectually. However, only in company does he become loquacious.

I have returned to college in the evenings to escape complete boredom.

ANSWER: Often those who complain that they have no communication with a loved one do not really know how to listen to the other with interest or patience. They merely want to be listened to.

Some use expressions of love for the other as a means of demonstrating that they are not getting anything like it in return. However, the basic message that gets across is one of criticism, which says that the talker does not feel satisfied or fulfilled. The one who is made to feel responsible for this vacuum in his mate's life then erects a barrier of silence, in self-protection.

Just as a girl learns how to be a woman from her mother, she learns how to relate to men from her relationship with her father. Yet, after childhood is over, it is not healthy for the father to continue to be the first and most desired male in a young girl's life. If she has never given up her father as her beloved, she will require that the husband carry on this emotional tradition, being always a beneficent loving figure who listens, encourages, comforts and treats her like a little girl even when she is a wife and mother. No more than a parent can be a friend to his children, can a husband take the role of friend to his wife. This diminishes the marital relationship, both in meaning and closeness.

Apparently, when your husband is listened to with respect and interest, he feels free to express himself. The fact that he is so loquacious on the outside proves how great is his need to be listened to at home.

Returning to school is fine, but that you are taking evening rather than day classes is naturally open to question. This seems like a way of punishing your husband by getting out of the house when he returns after a day's work. Also, being away at night, when your children might want to communicate with you while doing their homework or planning their social life on the phone, constitutes a real deprivation for them, too. You may also be withholding in other areas on the grounds that you are too tired after a day of housework and school attendance.

Making childish demands of your husband indicates that therapy, in which you believe, could perhaps be of great help to you. You ought to take courses during the day, so that you can be at home when your children and husband return. Perhaps if you all sit together to do your homework, it might open the lines of communication in your family.

When your husband sees that you are making every effort to learn both intellectually and emotionally, he might become less fearful about communicating with you.

II

While money may be the "root of all evil," the lack of it can sometimes bring on marital discord. The problem of the father/provider who does not provide enough is a common one. Ostensibly the mother/homemaker who fills out the team has a real complaint if her mate will not change or try to better himself.

However, in our society, marriage is not essentially an economic arrangement. It is a sharing in every facet of life. When the head of the household does his best, and more, to meet his responsibilities toward his family, as the husband in the case described below does, surely he can expect a certain amount of love and appreciation in return. If, after twenty-odd years of marriage, the share in his family's life which is granted him is strictly according to the amount of money he brings in, then money is being used as a means of emotional exchange. But it may also be to justify a diminution in sexual response, which sometimes occurs at this time in a woman's life.

LETTER: *I am forty-seven, the mother of two daughters, twenty and eighteen. My husband, over fifty, is our problem.*

Over the years he has been dissatisfied with his ability to earn. Yet he has never taken anyone's advice about improving himself. He was in business for himself. It was a total loss. Now, he is working for someone else at moderate pay, putting in long hours to make overtime money. He has never worked for an employer whom he liked. The result—a cranky man, who is either silent or sarcastic at home.

His attitude toward the girls hurts me so much that I have been ignoring him sexually for a long time. My daughters, both single, are very lovable types, but never go out. He is very cold toward them. His free time is either spent with the TV set or his coin collection.

What can be done with a man who will not seek help, will not discuss anything, or feel anything for his wife or children?

We have no money to establish separate residences. Do we continue to pass each other by in silence, in our four-and-a-half-room apartment?

ANSWER: Though it may be true that he has never made a great deal of money, your husband has evidently made enough through the years to support his family. He may not have liked any boss at work because he felt that he was already being bossed too much at home. Though he may not have liked his jobs, he has always taken a job and made a living. He is now working overtime to carry out his responsibilities to his wife and children.

Instead of getting appreciation and approval for his persistence, his hard work and his sense of responsibility, he is looked down upon and denigrated by the women in his family. Naturally, this is terribly discouraging to him and he withdraws into a world of his own and pursues his own avocational interests. There, at least, he can decide what he wants, and what to do with his time and energy. His withdrawal and his cranky behavior are ways of protecting himself from the criticism he constantly gets or expects. To leave himself open to your suggestions, is to leave open the door to attacks.

The very withdrawal which you criticize in your husband, you yourself practice in withholding yourself from him. Women who use sexual activity as a medium of exchange to bargain with, tell how little they really feel themselves to be women and how little they desire sex.

Sexual withdrawal is no way of getting your husband to pay more attention to your daughters. It creates an unwholesome psychological atmosphere and makes the girls indirect participants in the sex life of their parents.

Your husband will not go for help as long as he is made to feel the sick villain in the family. But if you sought some expert guidance, it would be an admission, which you really ought to make to him verbally, that you have contributed your share toward the poor relationship which now exists between you. This show of goodwill on your part will make him feel better about himself, and may give him the will and the strength to admit his own weaknesses and try to correct them.

Having an expert listen to him respectfully and hear him out, without prejudging or penalizing him, may encourage him to enter into calm and constructive discussions with his family, without fear of being annihilated. As you, on your part, talk about some of your own problems, you will find that the barrier of silence between you and your husband will become smaller and smaller, as well as your need to seek allies in your daughters. Then your daughters will feel free to relate to others and hopefully, in time, enter upon good and loving marriages.

III

Women of today have assumed active roles in many areas once considered exclusively masculine preserves. But there is one role which no real woman ever wishes to take on voluntarily, namely that of a substitute for the father and provider for the family.

The following letter presents a case which is classic in its outlines. It illustrates a kind of feminine dominance that many Europeans, for instance, believe to be more characteristic of American women, in general, than of their own women. The wonder is, however, how such a marriage ever came to be, and why it lasted for as long as it did. This couple's reversal of roles obviously originated in the early years of their marriage, and continued for two decades during which time it intensified. Finally, in the middle years, the worm turned.

LETTER: *I am forty, and have two sons, nineteen and thirteen. After twenty years of marriage, my husband has left me for another woman. We quarreled almost from the first day. But at least he lived with me and people couldn't talk about me.*

My home and children come before anything else. I have never gone to a beauty parlor or had a woman in to clean. I have always managed the finances, and saved enough money from his salary to buy a beautiful home. My husband had wanted the money for a business, but I refused and he has never forgiven me for holding him back.

He never lifted a finger to help me on his day off, so I decided to sell the house. We moved into a new building, but I wasn't happy there, either, so I bought another house, where I now live. He had left me three or four times before, but always came back after about a week, because he missed the children.

In the past two years, I noticed that my husband started to go out alone and gave me all kinds of excuses for coming home late. Our last quarrel started over his car. He wanted money to have it painted and I refused, because I didn't think it necessary. He packed a few things and left. I thought he would be back in a few days, but he has been gone about a year. He is asking for a divorce.

I have pleaded with him to come home, if only for appearance's sake, but he says he will never come back. He supports the children and myself very well.

I have tried to show my children what their father has done to us. The older boy has very little to do with him, but the younger one worships him.

He is living in sin with this woman, a divorcée with a child, and wants to marry her. He tells me she is everything a woman should be, but I know that he'll only wind up in the gutter.

How can I make him see the light? It doesn't matter to me if he only lives at home for the children's sake. Our rabbi has spoken to both of us and has advised me to give him a divorce. I can't see it.

ANSWER: There are two sides to every falling out. You see your husband's weakness accurately, but like most people caught up in situations of this kind, you fail to understand the role you played in this domestic drama.

If you were to spend a little time honestly analyzing your own actions and motivations, you would get a more rounded and truer view of the situation.

You seem to have always regarded your husband as an incompetent person, able to earn a good living, but not smart enough to handle his earnings. You treated him as if it was natural for him to subordinate himself totally to you and give you his all.

In recognition of his good behavior and submission, you rewarded him with certain physical intimacies. Surely you now realize, after thinking it over, that this was like throwing a dog a bone. The houses you bought were never his, although his money paid for them. His opinions were not listened to, and his wishes were not considered. You may not have realized it at the time, but you usually wound up doing exactly as you wanted.

Not going to the beauty parlor or not having household help may not have been such great sacrifices. This may have been your way of showing what a good wife you were. Perhaps you didn't want to beautify yourself because you might have had to yield to his desire for you. You may have felt the same way about household help. Your house was your citadel where you reigned supreme without even sharing the drudgery.

That he gave in to you for twenty years with only an occasional objection is a commentary on your husband. Being a weak individual he evidently wanted and needed the strength which is in you. But as time went on, your strength became a constant reminder of the weakness in himself, until finally, he was driven to break away. He had enough hidden strength left to fight against what must have seemed like complete domination. Without seeing what you were doing, you made him feel that if it were not for you, he would be a complete failure.

Neighbors' gossip seems to have been more important to you than his happiness. Even now, you do not seem to want him because you love him, but for your sons' sake. Yet by your own statements you have tried to discredit him as a father to his sons. However, their father's departure was probably not a total surprise to them. They have been hurt, both by their father's conduct and how you chose to present it to them. Actually their father's return, on the former basis, should that ever come to pass, would not help the situation as far as they are concerned.

The commandment, "Thou shalt not commit adultery" is more than an injunction against physical infidelity to one's mate. It is a commandment to keep the family, the cradle of civilization, intact and together. There are psychological and emotional infidelities against one's mate that may be worse than the physical lapses. These do not always show in the statistics of legal separation and divorce.

Any parent who talks against a mate to the children is guilty of three infidelities—to the husband, to the children and to herself as a woman and a wife. A mother who stands between her children and their father is unfaithful. She is also robbing her sons of the image of masculinity which they need to take their place in the world.

The only thing that might help to straighten out the relationship between you and your husband might be for you to turn to an expert for help. Only after you have derived some insights into your own motivations and behavior could you entertain any hope of altering your husband's decision.

The greatest change therapy would bring about is in the rearing of your sons. The problems of their parents should not be visited upon them.

IV

Marital problems that befall Middle Generation couples sometimes brew and fester for a long time before emerging into the open. The usual reasons given for the seeming restraint are the children. Mom and Dad cannot have it out with each other without injuring their young offsprings' tender psyches.

Later the marriage of a child may trigger an eruption. It may be some problem related to the newlyweds that causes violent disagreement between the parents. Sometimes, the mother, especially when the grandchildren begin to arrive, feels the pressure of the "dangerous forties" and gives vent to long suppressed resentments.

Unfortunately, such an outburst does not always clear the air or correct the maladjusted relationship. Quite to the contrary; it may not only make a bad situation worse, but it can affect the new family just starting out on its own, as the young couple described below found.

LETTER: *My husband and I, married twenty-five years, have a wonderful daughter, twenty-four, and a nice son of sixteen. We are both in our early forties. My husband has always been very jealous of my parents, the children and myself. To appease him, I give him my undivided love and attention and push my children aside. In recent years, I have realized what a grave mistake it was and made amends, which fortunately for me, have worked out fine.*

My daughter married very well and recently presented us with a granddaughter, whom I love dearly.

My husband is an ardent sportsman and loves cardplaying, which, on occasion, has kept him overnight at a relative's home. I never tried to stop him. I firmly believe that a man who works as hard as he does is entitled to some time for himself. Therefore, I cannot possibly understand his resentment at my staying at my daughter's home, at her request, for two or three days at a time, to help her with the baby. My son-in-law works long hours.

Recently, my husband made his displeasure very plain at my daughter's home. I have not spoken to him since. The children asked me to stay home, as he has first claim. I disagree. No one has or should have first claim. I haven't neglected him in any way. It's very hard for me to believe he loves me as he claims he does. To my way of thinking, when you love someone, you want to see them happy. Jealousy is not love; it's a disease which must be driven out.

At this point I am so confused and heartsick, I don't know which way to turn.

ANSWER: The absence of neglect does not prove the presence of love. Some kinds of attention make a spouse feel he represents a burden, and that doing for him is a duty that has to be gotten over as fast as possible.

Jealousy is normally a sign of insecurity, and the jealous person is one who feels deprived of something. Life has withheld his due from him and denied his wishes.

The mate of a jealous husband, while complaining about it, often finds this characteristic in her husband attractive. It makes her feel wanted, and diminishes her insecurities. It may even give her an exalted feeling to play such an important role in her husband's emotional life. Interestingly, when the husband becomes secure and confident, the wife may find it boring and begin to tease her husband by suddenly showing interest in others. If teasing him works, she may then shift to appeasing him. Actually, she cannot tolerate a calm and stable marital and familial relationship.

Your daughter's happy marriage and contented

motherhood would indicate that you gave her loving attention and consideration. This may be much more than you credit yourself with in saying that you pushed your children aside. You may have wished to remain the undisputed Queen of the Realm, with your husband in the position of Prince Consort. But even when his interests and hobbies took him away from you, at times, it still suited your convenience. It was also, in a more subtle fashion, a declaration of your own entitlement to free time away from him, when you wanted it. He perceives, and perhaps rightly so, that your lengthy visits with your daughter to help her are good rationalizations for being away from him.

Your husband does want to see you happy. But he doesn't want to be told by your actions that you are really happy only when you are away from him. There is a big difference between going off to a football game or to play cards, and going away from your home and your job of homemaking for a stretch of days at a time.

Your sixteen-year-old son must have some feelings about these absences, too. You could argue that a big boy like him can manage for himself, just as his father does, for two or three days. But he and his father could both reply that your daughter should be willing and able to assume the responsibilities of marriage and motherhood, as all young wives do.

When your married daughter and her husband advise you that your husband should be your first concern, they are quite right. When the parents' problems are intruded into their home, their own happiness is infringed upon. The help you can give is not worth the price, if they are made to feel that it is dividing your home, while they are so happy with their new home and family.

You really have enough time and freedom to pursue your own interests and activities during the hours that your husband is at business, engaged in sports or playing cards. Perhaps you are heartsick because you know that you were really responsible for your husband's proclamations of discontent. He has not rejected your daughter, and he loves her just as dearly as you do. He just wants you to accept your proper role with respect to him and her. Of course, in an emergency, her needs may be given priority, and he would no doubt agree and even urge you to go. But if these two or three day absences are merely to help her with the baby, she can, and should, make other arrangements and leave you free to do your job with your family.

There should be no conflict or confusion about the way for you to take. It is right back to your own home. Your togetherness with your husband will show your daughter that having differing interests does not divide, but actually enriches the mutuality of married life.

V

Alcoholism is one of the country's major health problems. It affects over eighty million people, if we include both alcoholics, and those who live and work with them. While some authorities today believe that there is a physiological factor involved, no one can deny that there is always a psychological aspect to alcoholism, and that it is just as much a part of the problem, if not more.

Men or women married to alcoholics face a kind of problem that is peculiarly their own. Usually, alcoholism in either husband or wife must be dealt with on a two-pronged basis, including both parties, if it is to be solved.

In the middle years, the syndrome may assume greater intensity and the relationship between the alcoholic husband and his non-alcoholic wife, or more rarely, vice versa, may deteriorate to the breaking point, or near it, as in the following case.

LETTER: *My husband and I have been happily married for thirty-one years. We've had the usual ups and downs, but no great difficulties until now. His drinking has increased so steadily that I believe he would be classed as an alcoholic.*

So far, he has always remained sober during his working hours. Weekends and holidays he starts imbibing about two hours after breakfast and continues until bedtime, and also evenings during the week.

All our friends would agree that my husband's intelligence and will power are far above average. This alcoholism is the first weakness he has shown in his character. I feel that it must be a form of escape from his work, investment counseling, which he has seemed to dislike—and refused to discuss—in recent years.

Though he is too reticent to discuss his problems with anyone, even me, I have insisted that we should move to the country, a small town, or any place where he will be happy. This doesn't appeal to him. He says he isn't physically up to working as hard as would be necessary in a country place.

Can a vitamin deficiency cause a craving for alcohol?

ANSWER: It is a deficiency, not in vitamins, but more likely in satisfaction of one's basic emotional cravings, that causes a person to revert to such infantile forms of gratification as alcoholism. This is, in a sense, a return to the breast.

In the mother-child relationship of such persons, a background of deprivation is usually found. The child often felt starved for a basic psychological vitamin—mother-love. Some people find less self-destructive means to make up for this basic yearning, when it persists into their adult lives and relationships. They may still use their mouths, to overeat, or to talk constantly.

If they are lucky, they will find as a mate a mothering soul who is willing and able to be on twenty-four hour duty, feeding them love and approval, along with food and physical care.

Underneath the passive surface of the alcoholic, there is a demanding and authoritative attitude. In such adults, anything coming into or out of their mouths is still endowed, unconsciously, with the same magical power as it was in childhood.

In the inner contest between desire and will power with which your husband is struggling, desire has won out for the time being. Whereas his work did at one time bring him enough psychological emoluments to make up for deficient rewards in other areas, this does not seem to hold true any more. Either the rewards have so decreased, or the hunger pangs have so increased, that they can only be silenced by the sedation which liquor provides.

Much as he may say he now dislikes his work, particularly as compared to former years, the knowledge that he is still functioning and making a living at it makes it much less distasteful to him than you think. He must still enjoy some status and a modicum of success there, for he does control himself at work. Its familiarity makes him feel at home there, and gives him a measure of security and control.

At home he throws caution to the wind. Perhaps it is because he feels he can take chances with you. On the other hand, it may be with you that he feels most deficient as a man and as the head of the household. If treated like an inferior and a weakling, he may punish you and tell you off by acting like one.

Perhaps also because he cannot make love at this stage of life as he did formerly, he feels unloved, forsaken and alone. When a man feels his lack of desire is evoked by his partner, he may begin to feel anxiety about his desirability, and be concerned about his potency. This decreases both his wishes, and his effectiveness when he does have desire.

This reality is much too threatening, and it depresses him. On the wings of alcohol, he can escape to the land of his dreams, without making a move other than to lift his hand and open his mouth.

Your suggestion of moving to a small town at this time must appear to him like a sentence of exile for having been a bad boy. Without friends and familiar surroundings, his feeling of aloneness would be severe and painful. Whereas his drinking can now be a rather private affair, no such privacy could be maintained in the more intimate atmosphere of a small town. To him, the move is like a threat of being exhibited in chains on the public square.

Dissatisfaction on your part and the disapproval of his friends is punishing, it is true. But it also serves to relieve the guilt that might otherwise drive him to better himself. Moving away to another environment would be only a substitute escape for the one he has chosen. It will not be a solution. It cannot dissolve his conflicts any more than alcohol does.

As for possible steps that can be taken, Alcoholics Anonymous does a rather effective job with some people who seek out this form of help and stay with it. Psychotherapy can sometimes benefit drinkers who feel great dissatisfaction and unhappiness with their habit. The combination of the two sometimes works even better than either, alone.

Vitamin deficiency is usually a result, not a cause of alcoholism. Drinking becomes the means of allaying both the physical and sexual appetites, and serves as a rationalization for the effect it actually does have of diminishing potency, while "it provokes the desire," as Shakespeare said.

The first step can be to go for a physical check-up from your family doctor. After the physical build-up, you may try injections of love and approval from you. He may then become strong enough to go for psychiatric help to rebuild his emotional health, and to AA. to control his habit.

✄ 7. CHANGES WROUGHT BY THE "CHANGE OF LIFE"

The smooth flow of life for a Middle Generation couple is sometimes dislocated by the occurrence of the wife's menopause, which is an inevitable physiological change in the life of every woman who reaches her middle years. The onset of menopause, coming several years later than it did just a generation or two ago, has a profound and universal effect.

But any woman who has led a fulfilled and happy life adjusts fairly easily to these changes, and usually does not develop any severe psychological problems. For a short and passing period there may be a slackening off of her love life with her husband, but in a happy and fulfilled marriage, the husband understands and does not take this as a punishment or deprivation.

On the other hand, to some women who have not had a happy life, or who feel that they have always given much and gotten little in return, menopause represents the beginning of the end of life. Although they no longer want to have children and are glad they no longer can, they fear that just because they are now incapable of reproduction, they will be rejected by their husbands, as they have been by life. If there is a change in their sex desires, this fear that their husbands will forsake them as wornout becomes even greater.

Sometimes, the menopause produces severe depressions or distortions in the woman's perception of reality, which require professional attention in order to bring her back to normalcy.

These alterations in a married couple's life can produce results which are not always predictable, such as a husband's changed attitude toward his wife, or a wife's changed feelings toward her husband.

Thus, menopause may not only be a milepost in the couple's married life, but may call for new compromises which must deal effectively with the realities of their situation and initiate a totally new period of adjustment for them.

I

One of the biggest hurdles that a woman has to get over at the onset of menopause is worry about whether the change will bring about a change in her relationship with her husband. Strangely enough, he has the same worry from his side of the fence. Although menopause is a physiological fact, there are some psychological aspects of it that many men share. Some psychiatrists are actually talking about the "Male Menopause."

The wife who wrote the following letter posed many of the problems that face women during this period.

LETTER: *I have heard what happens to women in their "changes." I never thought it would happen to me, but now it has.*

I can take the hot flashes and the feelings of discomfort that come at certain times. But what bothers me is that I feel so terribly unattractive. I still like clothes and have my hair done regularly, but it doesn't seem to make me look or feel better.

I am forty-eight, happily married for twenty-six years, with a married daughter living in another state, and a son who is in an out-of-town college.

My husband is a fine father and wonderful husband. But I must admit I no longer look forward to sex, and actually become anxious before my husband makes any advances. It kills me to see how understanding he is when I cannot respond. Then I begin to wonder if he isn't getting his main satisfaction elsewhere.

Will this go on until the end of my life?

ANSWER: The woman's adjustment in the period of the menopause is accompanied by great inner tumult. She is worried whether her husband will now want and desire her, as he did when she could bear children.

Also, for some, abstinence from sex during the menstrual period was seen as a prohibition against lovemaking because it could not result in procreation. But once it was over, there was implied permission to engage in lovemaking all over again. But somehow, with menstruation and the customary prohibition gone, the whole excitement and satisfaction seem to have been taken away from the activity.

There is no discounting the discomfort from the physiological changes of the menopause. But it is as nothing compared to how threatening the fears and apprehensions can be to a woman. If she feels she is not as desirable now as she once was, she may withdraw more and more from having a sex life. Sometimes this withdrawal is only a cover-up for her feelings of inferiority, and she means it basically as an invitation to her husband to woo and court her with even greater enthusiasm than he ever did.

Very often, a woman's thoughts about her husband straying at the time of her menopause are a form of self-punishment for withholding from him what he desires.

Actually, with each important change in life, even though residuals of old problems may crop up, the person is given another chance to redo and refashion her life. As long as a person remains flexible and amenable to change, she can fashion a longer and happier life for herself.

At this stage in your lives, a couple still as young in years as you are can begin to do things together which you could never do before. A woman can fulfill some of her frustrated dreams, like getting a college degree, going back to remunerative work, or working as a volunteer for worthwhile causes.

There is no question that when you are once again in the stream of life, you will feel better about yourself, and worthy of the good things in life.

II

Menopause may present problems to a woman that are neither easy to define nor to solve. Some women go through crises that are as painful psychologically as they are physically during this change in their lives. They may, like the woman in this letter, require some professional guidance to help them achieve a satisfactory readjustment, and avoid the shoals on which their lives could otherwise be grounded, or even wrecked.

LETTER: *I am a married woman in my forties with two children in college and a wonderful husband whom I thought I would never stop loving.*

I started working six months ago to supplement our family income, and because I was lonely with the children and my husband away most of the day. After three months, I found myself attracted to my employer, who is a widower.

I discouraged him at first, but then I found myself in love with him. He is a man in his late sixties, not good-looking, but I can't resist his charm. I've tried breaking up with him, but weaken when he insists we continue.

Now he tells me he cannot be alone and is getting married, but wants our affair to continue. I find myself acting like a schoolgirl. I cry every night at the thought of giving him up.

I thought of giving up my job, but I feel I will miss him even more, and am heartsick about not seeing him.

How can I control my emotions at my age, without causing all this heartache? I've just started my change of life.

ANSWER: Men, too, sometimes go through a kind of emotional menopause and manifest the same behavior as women. Some become depressed and withdraw from all sexual life. Others go off on a sexual binge, and sometimes not with their own mates. To them, this phase of their lives heralds the beginning of the end, and so they go into bouts of sexual hyperactivity to counteract these feelings.

Throughout a person's lifetime, whenever a new phase is entered into, residuals of wishes and desires that were formerly fully suppressed and controlled may crop up and become active again. A woman who has been a good wife and mother for many years, may, when this change occurs, suddenly want the tender loving care of the father she missed in childhood. She then begins to look for a substitute father-figure. When such a woman returns to work she begins to look upon her mate as a roommate with whom she shared both quarters and expenses.

When she is working, she feels again like a young girl starting out in life, and free to form new relationships. Also, her children's maturation makes her feel old, and this may drive her into behaving in a way that she would find most objectionable were her own children to do likewise.

This man is almost old enough to be your father. He probably wants a nursemaid and companion now, more than a wife.

The change of job you are considering is certainly indicated. However, such a change will not, by itself, resolve your problem. Hopefully, you are seeing a gynecologist about the physiological change that is taking place in your life. It might also be well to see an expert in the psychological field.

The guilt you are no doubt experiencing because of your illicit affair can cause real problems at this stage of your life. You would certainly be wise to stop seeing this man and sever all relations with him. A psychiatric counselor could then help you to return to the family you love and to the ideals of marital fidelity in which you basically believe.

III

Psychologically, adolescence and menopause have many things in common. Both mother and daughter are experiencing a physical change; one, by beginning to menstruate and the other, by ceasing to do so. In one, the ability to reproduce life is just beginning, in the other, just ending.

The adolescent girl wants to know if she will be wanted, accepted and loved. The menopausal woman anxiously wonders if her desirability as a woman is waning. Both have doubts and fears that center upon this new condition in their lives.

Teenagers are very much aware of what is going on between their parents and are generally deeply concerned. An adolescent girl, like the one who wrote the following letter, may feel a very natural kinship for a mother going through her menopausal period.

LETTER: *I am a girl of sixteen and my mother is forty-three. She is beginning to go through the menopause and as a result is displaying all of the misery that goes with it. She gets migraine headaches, flushes and weak feelings. Fear and depression follow that.*

How can my father and I help her through these crucial years? She is a most wonderful wife and mother and everyone loves her.

Is rest advisable usually, or should she keep very busy? She is always tired lately.

ANSWER: Misery is not the inevitable accompaniment of the menopause.

True, certain physiological changes do take place at this period, just as at the onset of menstruation. While the physical balance is readjusting, there may be some discomfort in every case, until a new equilibrium is reached.

But some people adjust to changes, whether within themselves or coming from the outside world, more easily than others. There are emotionally strong people who cannot stand pain, and psychologically weak ones who demonstrate an amazing fortitude in the face of it.

Sometimes open complainers show a strong displeasure with illness and a refusal to knuckle under and submit to it. Agitating about it also affords some people the relief they need, and helps them to regain the strength they cherish and to which they are accustomed. Others take suffering meekly, as their portion in life. In the punishment that illness brings, they find a pleasurable surcease from their hidden guilt feelings.

Just as the beginning of menstruation heralds a woman's coming of age as a woman, so does the onset of menopause announce the end of her physical creativity.

Will she still be as desirable when she can no longer conceive and bear children? This becomes of special concern, if conception was the main criterion by which she judged her value as a female in the past.

Women who, out of fear or reluctance, denied themselves and their spouses a larger family, may now be torn by guilt feelings. The menopause is felt to be a punishment for what they missed by their own self-denial. Now the gates of opportunity are closing and panic sets in.

Physical symptoms can be helped and pain can be alleviated by a doctor. Your mother should rest when she feels like it, and should not feel guilty if she does so often. Activity is a help only for those to whom it serves as an escape and distraction. Those who cannot naturally gird their loins and move into action, and do so only because of pressure from others, find activity doubly wearing.

Your father can help by being attentive not so much to her aches and fears, but to her as a person. The reassurance she needs from him is that she is as attractive, desirable and lovable to him now as she ever was, which with the years, he has come to know and appreciate even more fully.

As for yourself, you can perhaps be especially helpful around the house. In your attentiveness to her in this respect, it is important not to make her feel she is any the less competent as a mother because you are now as mindful of her needs as she was of yours before.

Any lessening of your normal social life should be avoided. It might make her feel she is hurting you, the budding female, by taking away what is now rightfully yours. Besides, when you react as a female who appreciates her femininity, she will have the fulfillment of knowing that she has passed on a good heritage to you, and start living and enjoying life again.

IV

Sometimes when an accusation of infidelity is expressed, the accused husband may be completely innocent of the charge. The question must then be answered whether the wife's accusations are based in reality, or stem from the psychological upsets that sometimes come with the menopause, such as imaginary projections of their own unconscious desires onto their husband.

LETTER: *After twenty years of happily married life and three wonderful children, what is a wife supposed to do when she finds out her husband is having an affair with another woman? Is this what life is all about, to give yourself wholly to a husband and children, and then to find yourself out in the cold?*

I have faced my husband many times with the sordid situation, which he constantly and strongly denies, saying I have no proof. Pleading, arguing and violence have gotten me nowhere. She calls up constantly under different names and guises, the last time from an upstate resort where she went without her husband.

My husband is good to all of us, and I can't, for the

*life of me, understand the whys and wherefores of a situation
like this. I have begged him to give her up or leave me. He
won't do either. What happens now?*

ANSWER: Sometimes menopausing women who begin to be
cold to their husbands and no longer feel very responsive to
them sexually, in self-exoneration, accuse their husbands of
finding satisfaction elsewhere. This may be projecting what
they would do if the situation were reversed, and their husband rejected their loving advances.

What adds a semblance of validity to their suspicions
is that the husband often goes along and cooperates with his
wife's lack of desire. Sometimes it is out of consideration for
her. He does not want to make her feel that because she no
longer desires sex, she is losing her femininity or her youth.

A husband feels less of a man when his advances are
not accepted. He blames himself, feeling that some lack has
suddenly appeared in him to make him less desirable. The
rejecting wife often does not understand this. She argues
emotionally, that if he really loved and desired her, he would
put up a fight for her, and stimulate her desire. A woman
who loses her desire, feels she is no longer desirable. Because
she can no longer procreate, she feels useless and without
any justification for going on. The woman may start a fight,
in the hope that after the excitement of the battle, peace will
be concluded in a sexual truce in the loving arms of her
husband.

Such a woman may see in any appreciative or responsive behavior toward her husband by another female, the
beginning of an "affair." By making him desirable to other
women, she pays him the highest compliment, and expiates
some of her guilt for treating him as such an undesirable
sexual object. When another candidate for the wife's position exists, she suddenly cares enough to fight to keep him.

Some men will try to excite a wife by implying how much they are wanted and pursued by other women.

If the telephone calls to your home are your sole evidence of your husband's infidelity, your conclusions are open to serious question. If such a relationship actually existed he would certainly forbid this woman to call at your home. If she persisted, he would end the relationship because it would certainly create more trouble than pleasure.

If there is any validity in your accusations, and it does not seem very likely, his other relationship is apparently not a very strong one. Since he denies the very existence of such a person, he cannot choose between your alternatives of giving her up or leaving you, since he wants to stay with you.

Both of you should seek psychiatric help. Neither fighting nor pleading will resolve the difficulty. Both of you need to talk out your problems, dissatisfactions and fears with an expert who is competent to assess what is really at the root of the difficulty. If your husband goes along with you for such help, this will constitute proof positive that he wants a healthy, happy you, more than anyone or anything else in the world.

⚜ 8. HAZARDS OF THE WORKING WIFE

In our time, the tendency for wives to return to work if they have had a career before marriage, or to seek some kind of employment, or a "cause" to which they can lend their services on a regular but volunteer basis, if they do not have any marketable skills, is much greater than in former times.

Women are healthier. Their child-bearing years do not take as much out of them because of their capacity and inclination to limit the number of children they have. The business world is much more accepting of women in many areas formerly closed to them. The rising standards of living, the spread of higher education to a larger percentage of their children, and the increasing numbers of luxuries that have become "necessities" to their families today, make it almost imperative for qualified women to add their earnings to the family budget. All these, and many other factors, are responsible for the increase of women in the nation's labor force today. It is estimated that since World War II, which made women welcome because of the labor shortage, the number of married women, with husbands also employed, who work, has doubled (from twenty percent to thirty-nine percent, according to current government statistics). This is aside from women in the lower economic levels of the population who must work because they live below subsistence levels, also widows and deserted women, who must support themselves and their families.

Naturally, family living is strongly affected when the mother goes off to work. It interferes with child-rearing and husband-wife relations, to some degree or other, but this is not the whole story. The working wife, out of the home, is vulnerable to the pull of possible romance with her male co-workers. Herein lies one of the greatest trouble-breeders for Middle Generation wives.

I

Not all husbands look kindly upon their spouse's sudden desire for a working life of her own, away from home. When a wife returns to work, she sometimes, in effect, enters into a new kind of relationship with her husband.

This next correspondent faces just such a marital situation. Like a loving and considerate mother and wife she is fearful and concerned about what it will do to her marriage and her home life. The best way to begin is by trying to understand the nature of the problem, and to foresee the possible reactions and consequences. Then she can make a wiser decision.

LETTER: *I have been married nine years, and have a delightful boy of almost seven. My husband is a fine man, a good provider, and a good father.*

I married rather late in life, but I was able to conceive after two years of marriage. I am now forty-nine. I do not look my age. This is my husband's first marriage, too. He is fifty-four.

Before I married, I taught school for twenty years. With a few more years, I would be able to retire with a good pension. During the past two years I have been active in the PTA and in community services. The principal of the school suggested that I should get a substitute's license. I did, but haven't made use of it.

My husband objects to my working (for pay). He states that if I go back to teach, even part time, it will be the beginning of the break-up of our household.

I have never shirked my responsibilities to him and my son. I love them dearly. I want to understand what his fear is—why he doesn't want me to "earn." True, he does very well financially. But his attitude confuses me.

ANSWER: The husband of a professional woman is naturally proud of his wife's accomplishments and, if he is secure and well-adjusted, has a higher opinion of himself because he could get a woman of this caliber.

After the children are reared, should she want to return to work, he understands her need and desire. It is natural for her to wish to practice her skills and make all the contributions she can in her particular field. But in some cases, the husband may see her return to work as a return to the first love of her life, which gives her greater gratification than he can.

When he gets over his first reaction of hurt, he realizes that, feeling more fulfilled as an individual, she can make a better life for all of them as a mother and a wife. A trained and competent woman who is made to stay at home doing work she feels is beneath her may feel deprived and frustrated. She is then apt to take out her anger, in one way or another, on the husband and the children.

Your husband's reaction is understandable to a certain degree. Both of you married later than most. He wants to have all of you, in every way, to make up for the years that you didn't know each other and weren't married. He sees in your return to work a possible return to the former life you had without him. To him, therefore, it may say that for you, marriage and raising a family was only a little temporary sortie. Now that you have had this fling into love and marriage, it is time to go back to your former way of living.

For the time being, it would be advisable for you to go along with your husband's wishes. He would see this as a sign of respect and, most important, as your acknowledgement that he is the head of the family. It says that he not only provides well, but rules well and exercises authority in the family soundly.

Given this reassurance, he may in time see it your way and give his approval.

II

A wife who returns to work after many years of marriage, may, like the woman who wrote this letter, feel somewhat unsure of herself. What effect will her employment away from her home have on her husband and children? This is a natural question which should be raised and carefully pondered before decisions are made and the step is actually taken.

LETTER: *We were married when we graduated from college. I worked as a statistician for three years until our first child was born. Now she is at college, and my other two children are in high school, one a senior and the other a sophomore.*

My husband is with a business firm, in the sales department. He does nicely.

In the last couple of years, I have thought more and more about going back to work. I have discussed this with my husband and he says it is entirely up to me.

I am bored staying home, but I must admit that I am a little frightened about going out to get a job. What effect will this have on my husband and children?

ANSWER: A woman who returns to work after a number of years during which she has married and raised a family is unquestionably starting a new kind of life. The routines and schedules of her whole family have to be changed accordingly in various ways.

When the mother has a particular skill or is a professional, the children and her husband are in many ways proud of her when she returns to work.

But on occasions, when they have an annoying or hurtful experience on the outside, they still want their mother around to comfort, encourage or advise them. Then, they feel that the mother is more concerned about herself and her fulfillment than she is about them.

The wife who returns to work sometimes complicates the picture by wanting to be treated as a co-worker, instead of a mate. She now wants to be waited on, as she waited on her husband when he was the only wage earner in the house, or she may require more help with the household chores, on the grounds that she is now a working mother.

When this is the attitude of the mother, then the work can hardly be fulfilling enough, no matter how financially remunerative it may be. If going back to work creates radical changes and tensions in the home, it will in turn affect her relationships both at home and at work and may rob her of the satisfaction she might otherwise get from it.

The woman who has been absent from work for a number of years, feels as if she were a beginner starting all over again. She feels the same agitation applying for a job as she did the first time, and the same anxiety about whether or not she will get it.

The woman fearing rejection may actually invite it by the way she conducts herself during the interview. She may take over, do all the talking and behave as if she were the interviewer. This says that if there is any rejecting to be done, she will do it.

Or else she may be apologetic and underrate herself, giving the interviewer no choice but to agree with her that she isn't good enough for the job.

Facing up to these possible reactions, which are normal and realistic, can help. In your field, in particular, there have been many new developments and great mechanical progress through the introduction of computers. You would no doubt have to take some courses to bring yourself up-to-date. These refresher courses are given at many colleges and universities as well as in private schools.

To prepare yourself this way will help you get rid of many of the anxieties which you may have about resuming your work and then make the return easier for you and more acceptable to your family.

III

The entrance of women into the professions to work side by side with men was undoubtedly a great step in the right direction for the entire female sex. Women make excellent doctors, lawyers, and journalists. Most of them successfully separate their professional and family responsibilities, and do not take the office with them when they return home.

However, in a family in which both husband and wife are active professionals, a special kind of problem sometimes occurs. It is customary for the husband to bring in the lion's share of their family income, for that fits in with his role as the head of the house and the provider. However, as this couple found, when the role of family breadwinner is reversed and the wife brings in more than the husband, the competition that inevitably ensues can be damaging to the marriage, unless honestly and wisely handled.

LETTER: *We have been married twenty-four years and have a son nineteen. We have been scrapping all of our married lives and were separated for fourteen of these years, when our son was age one through fifteen. He seems to be functioning well at college, despite this heritage.*

My husband and I are both professionals, each doing fairly well in his field, although I earn three times what he does. He feels the discrepancy in earning more keenly than I do, and defensively holds us back from enjoying the luxuries we can afford.

However, he is constantly hinting that I take him out, buy him things, or in some other ways assume what he has been reared to regard as the man's role. When it suits him, he tells me a woman's place is in the home (though he has never asked me to quit my work, and becomes panicky when I suggest that I might).

Things are pretty bad between us now. I prevailed upon him to go to a counselor with me, but when some of his errors were pointed out, he refused to return. So I stopped too. What shall I do?

ANSWER: Much has been said about the working mother and her effect on the children and the marital relationship. But in many ways there are different and sometimes greater problems created by a working wife whose field is the same as her husband's.

Although you may want your husband to do as well as you, you do gain a certain status from earning more than he does. Your financial independence constitutes a great threat to him. If he doesn't do your bidding, you are free to leave him any time you want. Actually, this basic fear became a reality during the fourteen-year separation.

The only way to avoid this problem is to plan a budget covering the scale on which you wish to live and then put your incomes together, as you put your lives together, without differentiation. When "his" and "hers" are written with dollar signs, trouble always looms ahead.

An insecure person often sees in the suggestion that he go for help the worst kind of criticism and the implication that he is mentally disturbed. To go to a professional means to have this found out and confirmed.

People who are fearful of therapy may go for a few sessions in which they begin to ventilate their angers and hostilities. But the moment they are confronted in depth with their own problems and what they may have contributed to the conflict, or are asked to look at the other's point of view, they stop going.

Both of you have contributed to the situation that exists today. If you really want to change it, then you should continue to go for help. This would say to your husband that you, too, were wrong at times, and that the fault is not totally his.

Most of all, it would be a sign of good faith and of your wish to make the marriage a happier one. He will then want to make an equal contribution toward the resolution of your problem and will return for the help he, too, needs. Your son, the "silent partner" in your therapy, may benefit most of all.

IV

Some defect or disability long present in a wife or husband can suddenly become a handy excuse for the mate to strike out in a new direction, and try to begin all over again with a new partner. That such a move can be contemplated by a member of the Middle Generation, after a marriage of many years duration, may come as a great surprise to family and friends. But, after all, it takes a long time for human relationships to develop and fall into an accustomed pattern, and an equally long time, sometimes, for the pattern to break up.

When a problem like gambling has haunted a relationship between husband and wife for many years, its very absence, beneficial as it may be practically, can be upsetting emotionally. The people involved, like the woman in the letter which follows, no longer know what a normal relationship is like, and can be thrown off-balance.

LETTER: *I am married twenty years and have two sons, fifteen and ten. I have worked for four and a half years for a doctor with whom I have become infatuated (or actually in love).*

We have never had any clandestine meetings, nor have we expressed or voiced our attraction toward each other, but every glance, or even touch, in working with each other has become meaningful. Working with my boss has become so much a part of my life that I can hardly wait for the weekends to pass. I love everything about him, his kindness, his skill, his humor.

For ten years my husband and I fought bitterly about money problems. He lost whatever savings we had on gambling. I loved him dearly and managed on very little money. But after these quarrels, all I felt for him was compassion. I love my children very much. My husband is a good father.

My boss is a good husband, wonderful father and the kindest of men. He is a fine doctor, and has a very large and wealthy practice. His wife was a wealthy girl. She is a wonderful mother and a good wife. I am fifteen years younger than she.

My salary is very good. My debts are almost gone. My husband doesn't want me to quit my job, as my salary has been a great help. When I told him I was tired of working, he scoffed and told me that he, too, was tired of his boss— but still wouldn't think of a change.

The doctor, too, is clean, righteous and a wonderful character. Once he tells me of his love for me, I know he will want a divorce. It would mean hurting her, her children, and my children, who love their father dearly. I am deeply religious and afraid and ashamed of divorce.

Shall I forget about him and start anew somewhere else?

ANSWER: The transference of warm and loving feelings onto a doctor is not an uncommon phenomenon. He represents the Great White Father who goes about curing all the ills and miseries of man, as if by magic.

During pregnancy, most women are somewhat afraid of having a baby, and find in the doctor's competence, kindness and understanding the reassurance they need. This is magnified if they feel they are not getting the consideration and recognition they want from their husbands.

In gratitude, and because of his naturally responsive and concerned behavior, the doctor is made into some kind of Superman, the epitome of all the virtues. Sometimes, women go even further and feel that they are in love with their doctor. This makes them feel unfaithful to their husband and disloyal to their child, even before it has arrived on the scene. In extreme cases, a woman may have the unconscious fantasy that her doctor is the father of her child. After the delivery, all this usually disappears fairly rapidly.

Such factors are seemingly at play in your emotional turmoil. You have a saint in the office and a sinner at home. You have had to help your husband provide for the home. When a gambler gambles with money needed for the comfort and welfare of his family and goes on one of these binges, he is like a child in search of the good mother he never had. He hopes to become the favorite of "Lady Luck," who will one day shower fortune upon him.

The wives of gamblers often play a much different role than is usual in a marital relationship, which includes a large component of mothering. They appear to have a basic need to dominate a weak male. Such wives will often take over and become the boss and supreme authority at home. However, the satisfactions from this do not always compensate for the burdens they have to assume in the process. They may then covet the normal female role, become unhappy, and start to complain.

The relationship that you have established with the doctor is entirely different. He is the boss and you are the subordinate, and you love it. True, you give him assistance in helping others, and he is dependent on you to get his work done efficiently and well. But, as the leader/expert, he gives the directions which you follow. Evidently, the doctor has evoked more femininity in you than your husband. Because you like yourself better with the feminine side of you in the ascendancy, you love what he has done for you.

You must, however, face realistically the probability that the feelings you think the doctor has for you are only a projection onto him of your own emotions. The wish on your part that he should reciprocate in kind is so overwhelming, that you push it over the line into a belief that it is really so. In your fantasies, you are, in a way, gambling in exactly the same manner as your husband gambles with the family's savings. Only this time it is with your family's happiness and security. The interpretation you place upon his glance or upon any accidental contact as you work together, may not tally at all with what he feels.

If he is the good husband, wonderful father and kindest of men, as you say, he would certainly control his desires, even if they were what you imagine them to be. He would not let them suddenly overturn the long-established pattern of his entire life and relationships. Such a man controls his impulses and practices renunciation for the sake of his life's values, and for the good of his family.

There appears to have been a marked change recently in your relationship to your husband and in the atmosphere of your home. He no longer gambles; he now worries about debts; and overdue bills are rapidly becoming a thing of the past. Perhaps you now miss the agitation and quarrels which added a spark of excitement to your life, and you have found yourself a substitute on the outside. Your unacceptable desires, centering around your doctor, provide a new excitement and give you a feeling of being alive again.

A change of job would help you to get over your infatuation with your doctor and forget him. But even more than a change of job, you need a change of attitude, to help you adjust to the more normal, peaceful way of living which you now have at home with your husband. This is probably what you long dreamed of and prayed for. Now that you have it, you should make every effort to like it and find satisfaction in it.

Perhaps if your husband were not made to feel inferior, especially now when his behavior pattern has changed to one much more mature and responsible, he would in turn take care of and appreciate you. He wants and needs to be truly accepted by you. You need not be deprived and assaulted, in order to be a real and loving helpmate.

Most important of all, getting some expert help could provide some clearer insights into your real wishes. This will enable you both to enjoy more fully the life you have built for yourselves so far, and to extend its horizons as far as you wish.

⚜ 9. THE UNFAITHFUL SPOUSE

With the so-called "sexual revolution," it is often alleged that there has come a general increase in infidelity on the part of both sexes. This phenomenon has probably not left the Middle Generation untouched.

Some men in their middle years, fearing that the passage of time has lessened their potency and their masculinity, suddenly seem to feel the need to satisfy two or more women at once, as a way of proving their virility.

Though, as a rule, fewer wives than husbands stray from the marriage bed, there is no doubt that some Middle Generation women have also been affected.

Women in the middle years no longer feel, as they did years ago, that it is unladylike to acknowledge their sexual desires, and to deny that their desires and pleasure are declining, or are not being met when they reach their forties. On the contrary, with menopause now coming some years later than in previous generations, and with the life-span rapidly increasing, Middle Generation women respond to the general climate of youthfulness and vitality of today's middle years. Some wind up engaging in extra-marital affairs.

Such women are spurred on by the feeling that, being emancipated, they no longer have to sit back and wait until a man makes overtures to them. They challenge what they regard as the old-fashioned idea that men's sex drives are stronger and more frequently aroused, and therefore demand greater gratification. They demand the right to meander from the "straight and narrow," just like men.

Yet, despite this so-called liberalism and the seeming social acceptability of the greater sexual freedoms of today, infidelity, when it rears its head, is still a wounding experience for one or the other of the marriage partners, and most of all for their children, no matter what their age. It still produces feelings of betrayal, deprivation and inadequacy, and strikes at the twin pillars of love and trust.

I

This is not only an age of sexual "liberation," it is also an age of greater psychological insight. Spouses today know, for instance, that a mate who is unfaithful usually wants to be discovered, even though there may be loud protestations to the contrary. The unfaithful one will leave clues around to be found by his wife, like a letter, a handkerchief, or a shirt with lipstick on the collar, which he knows she cannot miss. In fact, the unconscious "tip-off" tells that he wants to be rescued, as was the case in the following letter.

LETTER: *What makes me so mean that I cannot forgive my husband for having been unfaithful to me?*

I am in my early forties and have raised three fine children. The affection my husband shows me brings envy to all who meet us.

But, deep inside of me, I am disturbed with my false covering up of placid acceptance. My husband is evidently the kind of man that can "honey" and "deary" me, and yet carry contraceptives in his pocket, just in case.

*Believe me, I did not look to find out, but acciden-
tally came to know, and I have never felt the same toward
him. I never mention it to him, but when he travels for
weeks and comes back to me, I sense a distasteful feeling
within me.*

*I wanted to overcome this distrust, and so I built a
wall of forgetting. But try as I may, the suspicion crawls
through this wall right over to me.*

*I have enough outlets to keep me busy because I am
very creative. Yet I come back to myself with contempt. How
can we regain faith in those we love who have betrayed us?*

ANSWER: The explanation you have arrived at is not necessarily the only one possible. Yet, without permitting your
husband to present any explanation or to plead his cause,
you have passed judgment on him and made yourself prose-
cutor, judge and jury. This is not fair to him or to your
children. Neither is it fair to yourself, for you have made
yourself a victim, too.

The idea that your husband is unfaithful to you seems
to be bearable, as long as you can build "a wall of forgetting" around it. But you cannot bear to bring it out in the
open, because you may not want to find out why he has
strayed. When men seek sexual satisfaction on the outside,
the cause may not always lie wholly within them. Some
women seem to want and provoke a touch of unfaithfulness
in their husbands. In such cases they are both contributors
and participants.

Frequently the wife demands to be idealized and put
up on a pedestal. When sexual intimacies are expected by
the husband, it seems to blemish her purity. She may submit, but she does so with apparent distaste, or with shame.
The husband, failing to find fulfillment within his marriage,
seeks it elsewhere, outside the home.

To every child in his development toward maturity, his mother is both the pure untouchable goddess, and the woman who is his father's sexual partner. He must succeed in blending these two, to be able to choose a wife in whom the attributes of both are merged, a woman whom he can adore and idealize, and also desire sexually.

Many women seek rationalizations for avoiding sexual contact with their husbands—they are too tired after the day's housework and care of the children; it is unesthetic; there are finer and higher things in life; it is painful, and so on. Or else, they may find some flaw in the husband—he is not a good enough lover, or he is too passionate; he is not tender and considerate enough, or he is too much of a weakling to be attractive; he has halitosis, etc. Then it becomes the husband's fault, not theirs.

You say you love your husband and wish to regain faith in him. He must have earned your regard. You yourself say that his treatment of you excites the envy of all your friends. If only you could remove the blemish of suspicion, if he is not guilty; or bring yourself to forgive him, if he is, then all could be well again.

If your suspicions are confirmed, perhaps you will be able to investigate what led him astray and modify it.

If talking this out with your husband seems too difficult for you to manage by yourself, it is suggested that you consult a marriage counselor. Your marriage has too many positives in it to justify sweeping them all aside with the tar-brush of unproven suspicion.

II

The fact that an infidelity is practiced openly multiplies its impact on the rejected mate and the children involved and, for that matter, on the unfaithful one. Establishing new ties of love without first severing the old, as this man found, results in increased unhappiness for all concerned. The internal conflict within the wanderer can spoil whatever happiness the newer relationship could possibly bring.

LETTER: *What does a man do when his heart is being torn in two?*

I am married and have two wonderful children, thirteen and sixteen, who love me very much. I am forty-seven years old and have been married for twenty years.

Though my wife has been a wonderful wife and mother, we have drifted apart now for over a year. I met and fell in love with someone else and for the past year, I have been living with this woman. We have been very happy together, and I want to marry her, but my wife is lost without me and claims she still loves me very much and won't give me a divorce.

I love my children to the extent that I won't hurt either of them, and since my girl friend doesn't care if we live together without marriage, that's what we are doing.

I am all mixed up and feel not only love for this woman, but also very obligated to her, because she has helped me out with money and loves me very much.

I need help in my dilemma.

ANSWER: In mature love, consideration of the other is as important as sexual desire for her. Mere professions of love and assurances that one doesn't want to hurt the loved one are not enough. Actually such expressions are often used to allay guilt and to give the offender permission to continue behavior that does hurt the other.

Parental divisiveness, whether or not it ends in separation or divorce, is harmful to children, at any age. However, during adolescence, when they are more aware, and when they are beginning to feel sexual wishes and desires of their own, the violation of the marriage vows by a parent can hurt them more than at any other time.

But the greatest inconsistency is to talk about great love for them, and at the same time, to split the home apart. Children cannot understand why a father cares more for a newcomer in his life than for those to whom he gave life. The greatest danger is that they will finally become disillusioned and see love as a weapon with which to get what one wants, or as a trap in which to enslave others and make them do one's bidding.

The coming and going of their father keeps them feeling as though they are living in limbo. They are in a constant state of fear that the time will soon come when he will leave and not return. The unhappiness of their mother is certainly transmitted to them, and also adds to their confusion and their resentments.

The first area that such an atmosphere is likely to affect is that of their schoolwork. They find themselves less and less able to concentrate, because they are diverted and distracted by their worries and fears. Unfortunately, some youngsters begin to act up in the home and finally, on the outside.

Despite protestations to the contrary, you evidently do not want to divorce your wife and marry this other woman.

At this point, if you could repay the money that she gave or lent you, you would be free to make your choice without the "dollar dilemma." You could break up with the girlfriend and return to the family without feeling like a "kept" man.

It is good that you have finally come to see the situation as mixed-up and confused, and that you want to change it. At the beginning, being so wanted must have made you feel very masculine. But you are finally recognizing how undesirable the situation is both for yourself, your wife and children, and the woman with whom you live, too. Living with you, when she knew full well that you were married already, set the stage for the break-up to come. She founded her relationship with you on your unfaithfulness to your wife. She was betting against herself in imagining she could build a stable marriage on the shards of a broken one.

To continue to live in such a state of indecision for very long will create many more problems for you, as time goes on. They will become increasingly difficult to solve.

Evidently, the time to return to your wife and family is now.

III

It isn't always the husband who strays from the fold, though there are still far fewer straying wives than husbands. For the most part, women gain a favored social status when they remain as faithful wives and mothers. A working wife, however, may feel the need to prove her competence outside of the home. Sometimes, it grows into a need to have her desirability as a woman reasserted, as the following letter suggests.

LETTER: *I have been married twenty-five years and have two children, a girl of twenty-one, and a boy of eighteen who will enter college in September. My wife has been working for fifteen years, full-time for the past six years, and earns almost as much as I do. Her mother lives with us and takes care of the house.*

Three years ago she changed positions. Now she

spends even more time at her job, working late and having dinner with her boss. She claims she keeps him company because he doesn't like to eat alone. She insists she will not change jobs, and since I can't provide for all the family's needs, only she can make such a decision.

She puts in lots of extra time at her job with no extra compensation. Since she say she wants to get the most for her labors, I can't reconcile the facts.

I think the relationship has become more than one of boss and employe. I have asked her to consult a marriage counselor with me. She refuses.

ANSWER: A working mother is sometimes a better parent when she is fulfilled through her work in a healthy and creative way. When there is a real need for the mother to work, although the children may feel deprived by not having her with them all the time, they feel grateful for the extras that her work provides for them.

In such situations, the husband is bound to feel somewhat challenged. While he is happy to see his wife fulfilled creatively, he wonders why having children is not enough for her as it is for most women, and why he and the family are not sufficient to absorb her interests.

If the husband does not make enough to support his family in the style which the wife wants, he will feel inadequate when she goes to work to make up the difference. To make up for what he cannot give her financially, he gives in to all her wishes and demands.

A mother-in-law who is acceptable to the son-in-law can be a good person to take over the management of the house and the children. However, psychologically, this set-up can create problems. With the grandmother running the house, the parents become like a brother and sister in the family, each contributing to the support of the home. In such an atmosphere the wife may feel that, as a daughter in the family, she is free to build a social life of her own, and even to date someone other than her husband.

As her husband, you may have let your wife's behavior go on for too long. You only became upset enough to try to put a stop to it when it became obvious and noticed by others. It would seem that it is less her possible misbehavior that bothers you, than the fact that it has become public, even if only to your family circle.

It is hard to see what difference it would make if your wife were compensated for her overtime. She may well feel that what is most important to you is whether she is paid for her services, and not her misbehavior as a wife and mother.

Since your wife will not go for help, you ought to go. You will not only gain some insights into yourself, but also get the strength to take over and really be in charge of your family.

A feeling of unworthiness can make a person act in an unworthy manner. When she sees that you care enough to want to stop her and better the situation, she will feel more loved and therefore more worthy. She will then not need outside assurances, to feel loved and desired.

IV

Infidelity can sometimes be symptomatic of unresolved conflicts within the unfaithful one that are unrelated to anything the marriage partner has or has not done.

The woman who is the subject of the next letter needs, more than anything else, to understand her own inner motivations. When she gets to understand herself, she will gain some perspective on her marriage.

LETTER: *A very close relative confided to me about a very difficult decision she must make in the near future. She is forty-two, married twenty-two years, and has four girls, fourteen, twelve, ten and six.*

Her husband has always loved her, but she realized shortly after her marriage that she didn't love him as she wanted to. It has reached the point where she can't bear his presence and has no interest in anything he does. She likes people, likes to go out and have a good time. Her husband would do anything for the children, but doesn't particularly like to mingle socially.

A few times before this, she has reached out for happiness with another, but ended up with her husband, hoping once again that the marriage would work out.

Now she's met someone else, a divorced man who would like to marry her if she were free, and even take care of the children if she'd let him. He has grown children and says he was very unhappy during his first marriage. She would like to take what she feels is her chance for real happiness at last. But she doesn't want to hurt her husband by taking the children away, and doesn't want to lose them, either.

Her husband has always been aware that she doesn't love him, but he would be satisfied to go on this way. (He doesn't know about the other man.) She says that would mean she'd have to resign herself to a loveless marriage for the sake of her children. She feels that she could get to love this other man.

She is so upset about the situation that she gets moods of deep depression, has lost weight, and feels that she is carrying a perpetual burden with her.

ANSWER: This woman seems to find excitement and thrill only in the secrecy and darkness that cover up her illicit activities. The open permission which marriage gives to intimate love lacks the spark that "forbidden fruit" adds to her lovemaking.

Despite everything, she evidently does not want to give up her husband, more out of consideration for herself than for him or their children. What she really wants is a husband and a lover at the same time. She has not grown up emotionally enough to integrate the two into one.

The attachments to other men which she forms on occasion are short-lived because she only wants them long enough to prove to herself that she is desirable and can still attract a man, even though she is married and the mother of four children. Having gotten the lift she wants, she drops the "affair," and returns to her husband-father-figure. The rationalizations which follow are only to assuage her guilt for the irresponsible behavior that preceded.

Your relative is looking to be replenished with love by others, because she finds herself perpetually empty. Unable to give real and mature love herself, she blames her husband for it, arguing that if he loved her enough, he would evoke a warm response in her. The probability is that should she marry any other man, the same pattern or reaction would eventually recur. She would soon move away from him emotionally and find another lover, with whom she might have another affair, and so on, endlessly.

Her problem, which is deep-seated, is apt to go on unhelped and unresolved, until she realizes that she has a problem, and seeks professional help.

Quite in keeping with her pattern, she thinks she "could get to love" this divorcé, but does not love him yet. As before, she is ready to follow her uncertainty into marriage. She will marry first, and then challenge the husband to make her fall in love. The cart is thus once again put before the horse. Any new husband will fail, in all probability, just like her present husband. Nobody could succeed with this set-up.

Promises are very easy to make when there are all kinds of insurmountable obstacles standing in the way of their fulfillment. Having been unhappy in his first marriage, a man who is really looking for lasting happiness will find someone who is available for marriage, not someone already married. He will not choose a person who has to leave wreckage and misery behind her in order to join him.

Your relative is really looking for someone or something to bring out the femininity in her. Strangely, having mothered four children has not made her feel womanly, perhaps because the birth of each girl took away a portion of her womanliness, leaving less and less for her. She may see her daughters as competitors for male attention.

This last man is actually only another passing shadow in her life. The urgency to make a decision about him may come from fear that she will soon become too old. He is making a more serious proposal than any of the other men. This is making her face the realities from which she ran away when she ran after other men.

Her moods of depression are from anger with herself, and guilt over her immature acting out of childhood wishes. When physical and emotional symptoms begin to appear, it is time to take stock.

Perhaps if her husband were not embarrassed and humiliated by his wife's roving eye and seductiveness when out in social groups, he might be more willing to go out. If he is going to "baby-sit" to keep tabs on his wife, he would rather do it at home, and not under public scrutiny.

Confiding in you was a "cry for help" against her own impulses, which have brought her only unhappiness. She needs help to establish a sounder value system. When she likes and cherishes herself more, she will feel more loving to her husband and will be excited and fulfilled by him sexually.

🪶 10. MIDDLE GENERATION DIVORCE

Divorce is always a trying experience, regardless of how estranged the couple have become. It is a wrenching and tearing apart, overthrowing one's accustomed way of life, and beginning something new and untried. It portends for one or both of the partners a life of loneliness and frustration.

Divorce hits Middle Generation couples especially hard. Husbands and wives who have lived together for decades develop certain patterns which have the twin virtues, at least, of regularity and predictability. This provides some security not only for the husband and wife, but for their children as well.

Many Middle Generation divorces come as the climax of a long period of conflict. Very often the disagreements are kept out of sight and under control for the children's sake, during their formative years. Once the children are grown, the parents go ahead, assuming it won't affect them as much as it might have earlier.

This is, at best, only a partial truth, for every member of the family, even a married child, is affected. The pebble of divorce dropped in any matrimonial pond sends out a series of ripples that reach every part of the shore. No one involved is the same as before. The change touches everything and everyone.

According to the statistics of divorce, the peaks usually come during the first five years, and after eighteen or twenty years of marriage, when the children are well on their way toward maturity.

In today's Middle Generation, many who have had an unsatisfactory marriage feel they are still young and healthy enough to start a new life.

A husband may not feel guilty about it, for he reasons his wife is still attractive enough to start out again. Despite her hurt and rejection, the wife of today may not be as desolate as the divorcées of the preceding Middle Generation. She is not as restricted in her choice of a mate as women used to be, and she is more confident that she can strike out on her own and find a new mate.

The situation is worse, of course, when either partner asks for a divorce, after having fallen in love with someone else. This scatters far and wide the debris of guilt on one side, and hurt and anger on the other.

I

Generally, though children may catch a clue here and there, they are not really aware of what is transpiring until the time of the actual separation. Then, suddenly, their life is torn apart and one beloved parent disappears from the scene. The saying goes that one can divorce a spouse, but never a child; but from the child's point of view, this is a falsehood. The child feels assaulted, rejected, and divorced, in a way, by both parents.

They feel a great need for the missing parent and sometimes, paradoxically, their sympathy goes out to this one rather than to the one who remains and takes care of them. All their friends seem to have both parents and an unbroken home. Why can't they? What did their mother do to drive their poor suffering father away from home?

From this base, however distorted and unrealistic it may be, they ask the questions that can be lacerating to the remaining parent, who bears the brunt of everything, as in the case described below.

LETTER: *I am a divorcée aged forty-three, and have a boy aged four and a half. Due to unbearable circumstances, I left my husband while my son was eleven months old.*

Recently for the past few months my son has been asking for his father, where he is, whether he is alive, and why he doesn't come to see him.

His father never called or came to see him since I left three and a half years ago. He has three grown-up children from his previous marriage. The youngest boy, thirteen years old, whom he idealizes, was part of the cause for our breakup.

Occasionally, my son calls my brother "Daddy." My brother visits almost daily and plays with him.

What should I tell my son when he comes up with these painful questions?

ANSWER: When a loved one is lost through death, it is good to share the painful feelings of grief with the younger ones in the family. A child does not feel so small and weak when he sees the grown-ups suffering. While it may make the parent appear less powerful, it makes the child feel more so.

However, the loss of a mate through divorce presents a different situation. There is more anger and hostility than grief in the parting. A death is irrevocable, but as long as the two people remain alive, there is always a chance that there might be a reconciliation. Therefore, acceptance is not as complete and final as in the case of a death. While the spouse who wanted the divorce may deny the possibility that there will ever be a chance of getting together again, the children never give up this hope and hold it strictly against the parent who says no.

In any divorce, no matter who started the proceedings or won out in the end, each of the parties feels rejected. In fantasy, the mate returns suppliant and repentant, begging to be forgiven and taken back again. When this does not happen, the individual feels doubly rejected, and retaliates with even greater feelings of hate.

Mourning after a divorce may last longer and be more painful when a spouse feels guilty for having made a contribution toward the breakup. Instead of feeling happy with the freedom she wanted and fought for, she now feels alone and deserted, and as if she were being punished and victimized.

Apparently, you have told your son the truth, that his father is alive and well. The pain of meeting his questions arose when they went deeper than mere superficial queries. It is when your son introduced the "why" in addition to the "who" and "where" that you found yourself threatened.

While you accuse your former husband of having over-idealized the youngest child of his former marriage, he might accuse you of having penalized this youngster just for being around. Your underestimation and overcriticism of the child may have led the father to overestimate and overidealize him. Any child caught between two feuding elders may act up and cause difficulties.

Your negative reactions to the older boy may have increased when your child was born and you hoped and dreamed that your husband would redirect all of his attention to you and to the new life you had created between you. Ultimately, your disappointment became great enough for you to break up the marriage.

Perhaps all that you wanted out of the marriage was a

child of your own creation. Your inability to handle either the older boy or your marital situation after that may have precipitated your readiness to give up your husband. Yet, you must feel very guilty for having deprived your son of his father. Telling him all the facts is painful because of the revelations you must make about yourself, of which you are not too proud.

Your brother's presence and daily loving attention is an incomparable gift to your little boy. However, the very fact that he continues to inquire about his real father, and the whys and wherefores of his absence, shows that such a substitution isn't wholly satisfying. A substitute father-figure can help more in the absence of a parent through death, but it is more difficult when a parent is living and the child knows it.

It would be advisable, if at all possible, to try to work out a plan whereby the father can re-establish contact with his child. Perhaps for the sake of the child, he would be more inclined to agree. A father who is capable of such great devotion to one of his children, might respond to the need of the other, if he is given the opportunity to do so, without commitments or prejudice to himself. Perhaps the family agency of your religious persuasion can help to counsel you and ease the way. Meanwhile, tell your son, when he again asks questions, that although you and his father are separated from each other, you are united in your love for him.

Any adverse statements you may make about your former husband will wind up inviting such questions from your son, and may even turn him against you. This would be most unfortunate for all concerned.

II

When the children of divorced Middle Generation parents are in their teens or older and out on their own, they are, of course, fully aware of what is going on between their parents. Sometimes, they become involved themselves, taking the side of one parent against the other. When this happens at the instigation of the mother, who tries to turn them against their father, it can be especially painful. He suddenly finds himself, like the father in the letter which follows, feeling estranged from his children, as well as his spouse. After all, he reasons, he has not divorced his children, and he still loves them dearly. Why can't they at least be neutral?

LETTER: *After twenty-three years of marriage, my wife and I separated four years ago. Her reason for leaving me was the accusation that I was consorting with a widow who lived in the same house. I never spoke more than five words to the woman.*

My wife was beginning to go through her change of life, and sick, false accusations plagued me day and night. It was also very unpleasant for my two daughters, one twenty-one and now married, and one seventeen.

My two daughters haven't seen me for three years. I tried contacting them, but they ignored me. The court awarded me visiting days with my daughter, but you can't force a seventeen-year-old to see you.

I live alone, and have no life beyond my work and visits with my brothers and sisters.

How can children be so unfeeling to a father who only loves them?

ANSWER: Emotional complications and upsets, like the one between you and your family, sometimes do come from the gross misinterpretations and fantasies that some women suffer from during their "change of life." The picture that you present is not uncommon.

For some women the irrevocable changes of the menopause are fraught only with misery and unhappiness. Because they can no longer have children, they feel that they are worthless. The fact that they still have sexual desires and can function just as well sexually as before, is not taken as a triumphant fact of the ongoing force of life, but as a shameful regression which engenders unbearable guilt feelings. Only child-bearing justifies sex, and once this power wanes, the sex urge stands revealed in its naked sinfulness.

Even if sex never played too much of a role in their lives until now, it suddenly becomes infinitely desirable, because they think they have lost it forever. But they fear not being wanted any more, so they take the initiative by rejecting the partner, before he rejects them or becomes involved with another woman. By counter-attacking in advance, the woman thinks she can avoid the hurt she fearfully anticipates.

Most of this goes on entirely in her mind, but she cuts off all intimate relations. Under these circumstances, the husband could become unfaithful to her. She feels justified in expelling him, having made him into an adulterer.

An accusation of infidelity against one of the parents, particularly when it is unfounded, can be detrimental to youngsters' psychological development. The children respond to their mother's psychological upset by being protective and loving to her, instead of being fair and objective to both. Later, they may seek out the rejected parent and then re-establish the relationship on a warm and loving basis.

For the time being, there is probably little that you can do, except to continue to try to establish contact with your daughters. Writing to let them know what you are doing and how you feel about them cannot harm your cause. It can only help, provided you let your love shine through. There should, of course, be no recriminations against them for not responding to your overtures. You may also want to remember their birthdays and other suitable occasions with cards or gifts.

Their mother may need their support and partisanship at this time, but if you bide your time, they will very likely return to you.

III

Whether or not all marriages are made in heaven, it is certainly not true, despite a lot of modern propaganda to the contrary, that all divorces are made in heaven. They do not always bring the great relief from all emotional stresses and strains that is sometimes expected.

Very often the divorce, once achieved, sets off a chain reaction with one or both of the individuals concerned. The temporary relief may suddenly give way to second thoughts, which lead to many self-doubts and uncertainties about the wisdom of the action which was taken. This, in turn, can lead to the feeling that perhaps a mistake has been made, and may cause the now self-tormented ex-husband or ex-wife to start making efforts toward a reconciliation.

Sometimes it is too late, for the rejected spouse has remarried. Other times, considerations like pride, or the damage done through the public airing of the private quarrel, or the intervention of unforgiving family members, may prevent a reconciliation. When the regretful person finally gives up and begins looking around for a new mate, it is like accepting half a loaf, without the hope of regaining anything equal to what was lost, as in the case that follows.

LETTER: *Recently my sister obtained a divorce from her husband. She had married in her late thirties and has no children. This divorce was on her own volition, but had the backing of her family and family doctor.*

However, she speaks longingly of her marriage and defends her husband at every turn. In fact, she gives you the impression that she did not do the right thing by getting a divorce, and yet she was the one who took the step.

She is pessimistic by nature and has always distrusted men, and now that she is single again, finds it a great effort to get back into circulation. However, she is very anxious to remarry as she finds her present life lonely and unfulfilling.

I try to remind her that it is preferable to be single, rather than unhappily married, but she says that every marriage is unhappy.

ANSWER: The only difference between your sister's reaction to her divorce and that of many other divorcées, is that she is admitting out loud what some others keep strictly to themselves.

There are always some regrets after a final separation. It spells the end of a phase in one's life and is felt, at the time, to be as irrevocable as death. In the period following the legalization of the break-up, the divorced person often goes through a period of mourning, similar to that after the death of a close one.

The divorce gave them permission to terminate the objectionable or hated elements in the marriage, but once separated, the positive memories somehow return. The sum of these sometimes looms larger than was originally appreciated, and is magnified by the feeling of loneliness which now prevails. Regret may trigger an attempt at reconciliation, and in some such cases, remarriage does work out better than the original union.

A woman who does not marry until her late thirties usually has a basic fear and unreadiness for marriage.

This is not overcome by a brief excursion into matrimony. She may be persuaded to do what society and her family expect of her. Having proved her point, she breaks up the marriage as soon as she can reasonably do so.

Though she is in her forties, your sister evidently still regards herself as the dependent problem-child of the family who, although she did exactly as she pleased in getting married and getting divorced, now turns on her family and blames them for not stopping her, beforehand, and for letting her go on with it, afterward. They may not even degrade or malign the one she has rejected, lest they incur her wrath. This is, of course, an absurd position.

Building up her former husband has the sole purpose of giving herself a build-up. With this encouragement, she may then convince herself that next time she will do even better. Your sister hears your reminders that single bliss is to be preferred to marital unhappiness as an adverse judgment of herself.

Her distrust of men will not make men more trusting of her. No man wants to have to prove his trustworthiness in a courtship. The only proof he wants is that the woman he desires finds him desirable.

Your sister's wish to remarry reveals not pessimism, but a greater optimism than her family perhaps appreciates, despite her overt statements. Her actions, in this case, speak louder than her words.

Perhaps your family doctor who was so sympathetic to her in her desire for a divorce, can now be a sounding board for her renewed desire for marriage. If he deems necessary, he could recommend a psychiatrist who could help your sister work out the feelings of inferiority she has about her desirability and acceptability. These are probably at the root of what makes men appear so uninviting and unacceptable to her.

Should she then decide that marriage is really not for her, it will help her to live with herself. She can then fill her life with absorbing interests and fulfilling friendships, such as she has not yet enjoyed.

11. DEATH CUTS THE GOLDEN THREAD

The death of a husband or a wife is felt more deeply, perhaps, by members of the Middle Generation than by others in older age brackets. Increased longevity and improved health standards have given the Middle Generation an added measure of comparative youth. What crueler fate, therefore, than to have one's mate taken away forever in the prime of life.

No person can conceive of his or her own death. Death represents a desertion, as if the early childhood fear of being abandoned by one's parents for being bad has come true. On the other hand, the guilt people feel about the deceased often stems from deep-seated feelings of relief on the part of the survivor for having been spared.

When a married couple has reached old age after a long and happy life together, separation by death, hard as it may be at the time, is more easily acceptable as an inevitable fact of life. There is a period of loneliness for the survivor, requiring certain attentions from grown children, even though they are now parents or even grandparents, in their own right. At an advanced age, it is not narcissistic, but realistic to admit that one needs help at a time of distress.

When one member of a present-day Middle Generation couple dies, the survivor's reactions may be somewhat different than in the past. At first, he may feel, typically, that he will never marry again. Then, as the period of mourning approaches its end, he becomes restless and complaining. It is his way of facing the possibility that he may really want to build a new life, after all. But he may fear that he will not be wanted by anyone.

Finally, his mourning period over and his grief assuaged, he is ready to make a completely healthy adjustment to on-going life. He moves out into the world again, fully prepared to take on new relationships. In a sense, by overcoming his sense of loss, he has conquered death.

More and more, this is becoming characteristic of bereaved Middle Generation members who do not passively accept permanent widowhood as their lot while they are still young, and want to build a new and different life.

I

One of the most agonizing situations anyone can face is the lingering illness and inevitable death of a husband or wife who suffers over a long period of time.

To see a loved one wasting away gradually over a period of weeks or months is a fearful strain, while day after day one is expected to maintain a brave front. This is especially difficult to carry off before the dying person, pretending belief in an eventual recovery that one knows can never be.

At the same time, there may be children to care for, a home to manage, or a living to earn. Under the pressure of these almost unbearable stresses, it is to be expected that sometimes, something will give way, and the most loving spouse or child may display seemingly bizarre and unaccountable behavior. Here is an interesting example of this phenomenon.

LETTER: *In my work as a nurse, I have seen a psychological phenomenon I cannot understand. It is now occurring to a friend of the family.*

In each case, the people involved are devoted couples who have been married for from twenty to thirty years and in each case it is the husband who is or was in the terminal stages of cancer. The husband and wife suddenly become estranged over some trivial argument and reach the point where the husband absolutely refuses to see the wife. In each case, the patient's condition worsened after visits from the wife.

One patient refused to eat, to the point where he suffered from malnutrition. Upon removal to the hospital, when the wife did not visit, his condition immediately improved.

The wives, instead of helping their husbands in their last living crisis, are consumed with self-pity and just about leave their spouses to die alone, after a long lifetime of happiness.

Is there anything one can do to make these last days of a dying man happier, or to bring a couple together again before it is too late?

ANSWER: The phenomenon you have observed, though a bit extreme in its manifestations, is not peculiar to this illness nor to the husband-wife relationship.

In people's reaction to illness, we can see a re-enactment of some aspects of their emotional life-cycle with their close ones in childhood.

A regression to infantile and childish mechanisms is normal during the height of an illness. There is petulance, whining, demanding behavior or altogether a pathetic dependency and passivity. This is usually given up once the crisis is over and convalescence begins. The individual gradually retrieves his controls and moves forward again to the more accustomed patterns of adulthood. Other people in sickness suddenly become bold heroes or patient and long-suffering martyrs, showing a strength that was never apparent in normal times. Sometimes buried hostilities come to the fore. The sick one now finds it safe to attack, for his very weakness spurs the conscience of others and stops them from counterattacking.

On the opposite side of the coin, the physically healthy one, who has always quietly submitted to domination, may now be emboldened to retaliate on the prostrate opponent. Either by thoughtless or cruel conduct, or by calculated oversolicitous and mournful care which reflects the hostility underneath it, she whips the sick one into a state of fear and anxiety about himself.

Most often, however, the real love and consideration, which was somehow hard to express articulately in good times, comes forth in full blast in such unhappy, fearful times. Individuals may then become closer than ever before.

Fear of death is an agonizing thought, rarely if ever shared with the sick one by the healthy ones. Thus, an impenetrable barrier is erected, against which the sick one batters in vain. He feels something is being withheld from him and that he is already being excluded from the inner circle of the living.

He watches like a hawk the facial expressions, the side-long glances, or the suggestions for future care to be given him, for some hint about his condition and his prospects for life. Circuitous means and tricky devices are employed to catch the beholder unawares. A big argument breaking out over some small unimportant detail merely reflects the really big battle waged underneath.

In the desperate fear and apprehension of the prospective survivors about death, there is already a preparation for the leave-taking. The mortally ill person, however, while unconsciously knowing his fate is sealed, consciously feels that he is being deserted by his loved ones, who are creating a wall of silence around him.

In his desperation, he often blames his plight on those who are trying hardest to be helpful. The "know-nothing," money-mad doctors, or the ungrateful wife and children for whom he slaved all his life, are now held responsible for this state of affairs, which they should have anticipated or avoided.

The state of not knowing increases his irritation. He doesn't want to go alone, and fantasizes that if his mate really cared, she would go along with him. An argument over some unimportant issue is only a rehearsal for the final separation which they both know is coming.

In medical circles, there is much discussion about the advisability of informing the patient about the inevitable outcome of his illness. But the patient, by his demeanor, is telling the doctor and all that he already knows.

While being sent to a hospital to some degree frightens the patient, he simultaneously feels protected by the institution and its workers. More relaxed, he becomes more willing to follow their instructions. Beside, this is his last outpost, and he cannot take the same chances with rebellious behavior here as he does at home.

While patients like thoughtful attentions from the world outside, visitors do weary them and leave them depressed. The contrast of illness is emphasized by the health and freedom to go and come of the visitors. With those close to them, each leave-taking may seem, unconsciously, like a rehearsal of the final separation. Both the patient and the loved one feel this. To fight makes life appear more normal, and seems like taking out insurance against the coming of death.

Such a wife needs to be given understanding for all that she is going through psychologically. To a sympathetic ear outside of the family, she might be able to express her grief and the loving concern she really feels for her husband. She might then be freed of her hostilities and able to express kindlier feelings toward him.

II

Most people react in an almost predictable way after the death of a mate. Once the shock of the loss is over and the vivid pain has receded somewhat into the background, there comes an interim period when the survivor is poised between deep mourning and the beginning of recovery.

During this transient period, it is sometimes very difficult to make the right decisions necessary for a healthy readjustment. A certain self-awareness must first be attained, and one must have developed to a point of readiness to take up life again.

The prolongation of mourning or too quick a recovery, both indicate deep guilt feelings about the survivor's relationship with the departed.

LETTER: *I lost my husband about five weeks ago, after being married to him for twenty-five years, and can't get myself to accept the fact that he is gone.*

We were very close and very attached to each other. Having no children, everything was centered on him. He was a very fine, warm, kind man who made me feel very good. I let out my maternal instincts on him. He made me feel wanted and he loved me very much. I now feel such an emptiness in my life.

I stayed on in the apartment we shared, and everything reminds me of him. I feel this awful emptiness every-

where I turn. I am working as I did previously, but coming home evenings, I miss him terribly.

I feel so bitter looking at people in the street who are much older, and saying to myself, why did my wonderful husband have to die while they are living? I feel so guilty.

Does one recover from something like this? I feel such a void in my life. How can I get back to normal living?

ANSWER: Grief is a very personal thing. Yet people's reactions to the loss of a loved one are very much the same everywhere, and there is a certain universality about the feelings of love and hate, and also of guilt, which it engenders.

After twenty-five years of a happy relationship in marriage, it would be abnormal for the survivor not to have a very hard time accepting the change and adjusting to it. Since the death of a close one is always felt as a personal assault, it is also natural for the bereaved one to have feelings of anger and resentment. But it is dangerous to be angry with the Divine Power or the fates responsible for the death. Hence the person in sorrow directs the anger and resentment at living targets.

Jealousy may also enter the picture, since if anything is to be taken away from her it should be taken away from everybody else also. The person may also express again the childish interpretation that life is a reward and death a punishment.

Anger may also be felt against the dead. Failing to overcome the illness and survive is seen as due to a lack of love, not to human frailty. He should have put up a better fight for life, and for her. These thoughts are as natural as they are irrational, and it does not help much to realize how illogical they are.

The survivor does not like herself when she has these

jealous thoughts, and feels almost like the Angel of Death in her wishes. She is sure that no one will ever want her again in love and marriage, because of these thoughts.

The pain of your loss may be even greater because you meant so many things to each other, above and beyond the relationship of husband and wife. You were like a mother and a daughter to him, and he was like a son and a father to you. With him gone, all of these roles have passed away, too.

Your call for help after five weeks indicates real progress in your mourning. You have accepted your husband's departure more than you can admit now and are already beginning to glimpse a future life for yourself. Right now, such contemplation can be frightening, and as a defense reaction, you are aware only of your feeling of anger. It is easier to be angry than anxious. To hit out at people is easier than to be hit at by fears.

Your first move should be out of the apartment in which you lived with your husband. To expose yourself continuously to the painful memories which the familiar objects in your home must evoke is to punish yourself for being alive. This prolongs your grief unnecessarily.

The second step is to change your activities, both inside and outside the home. Your maternal drives could perhaps be directed toward physically and emotionally handicapped children in hospitals and clinics. Participation in a cause in which you believe would take up your time and energy and give you the feeling that you are contributing to the continuation of life.

Last but not least, you should begin to socialize, and if possible to entertain those who have been kind and helpful to you. This will not only get you return invitations, but will make you feel right about accepting them.

When you give to others, you will not feel so guilty

for continuing to enjoy the gifts of life. They are really your due.

III

If young children are involved, the surviving husband or wife has a most difficult adjustment to make within the family. The breach in the close, secure family circle needs to be closed up and security re-established. The absent parent's ministrations in the children's daily routines have to be replaced with suitable substitutes. The sense of loss and frustration of the survivor are helped to be overcome or pushed aside by the demands of every-day living of little ones, upon whom one cannot foist one's problems.

Nevertheless, handling one's own frustrated personal needs and desires is the dilemma of many, like the woman who writes the following letter.

LETTER: *My husband died after a nine-month illness (cancer of the pancreas), after a marriage of sixteen years. Part of it was blessed with real happiness. We were at times extremely compatible sexually, and every other way. We had three lovely children, for which we were both ecstatically happy.*

My problem is my older boy, twelve. (The next child is a girl who tries to please me, and a little boy of eight, who is no problem.) He is big physically, eats with zest, and too much. I've never limited the amount, though I have, in a temper, called him "a fat pig." Sometimes we are on excellent terms.

This morning we had a battle. I struck him and he retaliated by striking out at me. This is not the first of such tantrums. He told me he had brushed his teeth, and he hadn't. I did it for him, with much temper on both sides. His hands were not clean, nor his neck.

After much threatening, I've arranged to send him for the eighth grade to a private school where he will have male teachers. He welcomes the idea, but in anger. He has female teachers now and is not working to capacity.

He only wants to play ball and watch television, and seems unable to keep his own room tidy. As for any household chores, it is a losing game.

I feel so futile and inadequate. I must admit I need sexual fulfillment. I am forty-seven but show no sign of menopause. I work very hard to forget my husband and my physical needs.

ANSWER: A parent who wants consistently good behavior from her child cannot be inconsistent in her demands and treatment of him. Every parent has the right and privilege to get angry sometimes, and even to let her frustrations and deprivations show. But it cannot happen too often, with one particular and specially singled-out target, lest he retaliate with anger, in self-defense and self-protection.

You are probably directing to your son, now the oldest male in the family, some of the emotions you once channeled toward your husband.

Just as some of your times with your husband were ecstatically happy and some not so compatible, so it is with your son. For a while you get along very well together. Then you have a fight—only with your son, you call it a tantrum.

Children your son's age couch everything in the extremes of too much or too little. They overeat, overtalk, overplay, understudy, and most serious of all, underrate themselves. But they understand more of what is going on around them than most adults are aware of or give them credit for.

In this wavering, they are trying to come to terms with

themselves and achieve a norm which is maturity. A parent cannot expect grown-up conduct from a youngster while treating him like a baby who has to be scolded, directed, wiped and cleaned. This does not permit the parts of his personality to weld together and become a whole.

At your daughter's age, it is appropriate for her to try to please you. She feels with you, because she too lost the most important male in her life. The youngest boy hasn't yet reached the age when the fight for independence begins, but you can expect the same reaction as from your older boy, later on.

Your youngsters cannot ever fill the physical and emotional voids created by the death of your husband. If expected to, they will respond by behaving childishly or by doing badly in their schoolwork, social adjustment, personal responsibility, etc. This is their way of saying that they are too young and inexperienced for the task you require of them.

Arranging for your son to attend a private school where he will be exposed to male teachers and guidance should be good for him. But you are using what is really a reward as if it were a punishment. This could frighten him about an experience to which he should look forward with pleasurable expectation.

Concentrating all your attention and energy on your children will not provide what you want and need for yourself. You should begin to build a social life and perhaps become active in causes or associations at your church or the schools your children attend. You cannot fight the lonely vacuums in your daily life by fighting with your children. However, when they see you occupied and happily absorbed in worthwhile activities on the outside, your youngsters will feel better and may want to help you inside your home.

Your sons should find in their men teachers, ministers, or relatives, males with whom they can identify. Perhaps when you have let go of your children to fill your needs, you will more easily find a man of your own, in marriage and self-fulfillment.

IV

A protracted state of mourning is one of the great dangers facing a widow or widower. A good marriage will not evoke feelings of guilt in the survivor, who will observe a normal period of mourning and is likely to remarry.

Unless this is understood, erroneous interpretations may be placed on the facts of appropriate recovery and resumption of life versus lingering in widow's weeds. A bad wife sometimes makes a good widow. Her guilt for the sins committed against her husband, keeps her in a constant state of mourning. She is loyal to him in death as she never was in life. Then, feeling like a bad child rejected by life, she wants everybody to mother her and wait on her, as if she were recovering from an illness. This letter is classic.

LETTER: *I am a widow of eleven months. I seemed not only to lose my husband, but all my friends. I am amazed and bewildered about this sudden change. They were my friends, as well as my husband's. Why, when I need them the most, now, are they so strange? Is this natural?*

Because of this, I intend to change my environment and move to another neighborhood. Am I right in moving?

ANSWER: Statistics show that there is a higher percentage of remarriage among divorcées than among widows.

There may be criticism about how the divorcée handled her first marriage, but people usually feel free to introduce her to available men and to set up blind dates for her, because they know she is ready and eager. The divorcée does not have the sense of loyalty that the widow has to the man who once was her husband. Usually, her emotional attachment has been broken for a long time before the divorce, so she is free to relate to another man.

If the marriage was a good one, the widow will look around for someone to equal her first love, when she feels ready to remarry. A man who begins to date a widow often feels that comparisons are always being made, and he keeps wondering what his rating is. However, the man who dates a divorcée feels that he begins the relationship with a head start.

Every widow sees the death of her beloved as some kind of deprivation or punishment of her. She often feels that those living around her should make it up to her, and she expects all the overtures to be made by them.

The other side of the coin is that the widow is afraid to take the initiative for fear that her invitation might be rejected. So she sits back and waits for the invitations to come. It is difficult in many ways to be a hostess without a host.

At first, the family and friends are mindful and considerate, and do everything possible to be of comfort and help to the bereaved. But when her needs are excessive, go on for too long, and undue demands are made on them, friends and relatives slowly but surely begin to shy away and see less and less of the widow. Her hurt leads her to withdraw more and more.

That your whole circle of friends and relatives seems to have moved away would suggest that it is you, not they, who caused this separation. It may be their way of suggesting that you begin returning to normalcy.

The first step would be for you to show the same consideration and mindfulness of the needs of others as you did before your loss. People instinctively veer away from those who view life with bitterness and resentment. Moving to another neighborhood with this same attitude could only create the same situation with the new friends. You ought to begin to invite your old friends over and start entertaining again.

This would help to re-establish your friendships on a giving as well as a receiving basis, and would make them want to include you once more in their social life.

Seeing that you fit into the picture of their normal social life, and that you can be cheerful and pleasant, they may even begin to invite available single men as escorts or dinner partners.

V

To some people, death seems to become a regular partner in their lives. No matter how well they adjust to the loss of one mate, a second such loss seems devastating. To pick oneself up and try to make still a third marriage takes a great deal of courage and understanding, as this woman is finding. A big hurdle is to overcome the superstitious belief that some kind of malevolent fate is dogging her footsteps.

LETTER: *I am a woman in my late forties. I was first married at eighteen to a wonderful husband. We were very happy together for ten years. He was then taken very sick, suffering for several years, and then I lost him.*

After some time, I met a very fine man and remarried. This man also took very sick after twelve years of happiness together, and died. I gave all the care I possibly could during their illnesses to both my husbands.

I never had any children and find my life now very

empty and lonely after being needed and loved by two wonderful men.

My friends and relatives tell me I am still young and attractive. I somehow look upon a third marriage as shameful.

ANSWER: People of all ages need to love and be loved. Those who have the qualities of goodness, kindness and understanding will always be attractive and desirable to others.

There is nothing shameful in admitting this capacity and this need to share one's gifts in a loving setting.

You were not disloyal to your first husband when, after his death, you found love and marriage with another. The devoted care you gave to both, without bitterness or recrimination, no doubt prolonged their lives. Nor did you take anything away from your first husband when you cared for your second husband.

When great sorrow or deprivation comes, people often do a lot of emotional homework in search for an answer to the great mystery of "why did this have to happen to me?" Sometimes in this process, they turn on themselves and mercilessly hold themselves responsible for the sad fate that has befallen them.

You are not a failure because you could not prevent, protect and rescue your husbands from their serious and fatal ailments. Your second husband was not taken from you in retaliation because you remarried and loved him, as you did your first.

Women who are able to bear children are often better able to accept a remarriage, gaining also a new father for their little ones. This provides a handy self-justification and a palliative for any guilt they may feel about it. Sexual desires and intimacies also seem less shameful when they may result in the conception of a child.

Having had no children with either of your husbands

when you were younger, remarrying a third time, when the chances for conception are even less, may highlight your embarrassment. It may represent a blazoning forth of the two secrets you had hoped to keep from the world, that you may have been the cause of the childlessness, and that you married nevertheless, to give and receive love.

But this is not a shameful revelation. Rather, it proves how a psychologically healthy person can find happiness through substitute fulfillment, remaining attractive in spite of handicaps.

You must surely recognize the purely coincidental character of the ending of your two marriages. This must not be construed as a destiny which has been assigned to you, or a pattern that will continue to be followed.

You can still contribute great happiness to another, and partake of your share of it, yourself. The only shameful thing would be to withhold this from yourself.

12. THE HEALING BALM OF REMARRIAGE

One of the happiest changes which is taking place in the lives of Middle Generation people today is the general approval of society when they display a readiness and general willingness to marry again, following the death of a mate. This was not as true in the past, when widows, at least, often resigned themselves to a state of singleness and loneliness. Now, once the shock of separation is over and the necessary adjustment has been made to the unaccustomed single state, the need for companionship and love and for a fresh start in life begins to assert itself, and is respected. For a widow or a widower whose first marriage was a happy one, what could possibly be more natural than that they should eventually develop a strong urge to recapture the same kind of experience with a new partner.

With divorcées on the other hand, the marital experience having been an unhappy one, they may not be all that eager to try another round. The exception is, of course, where the divorce was caused by one spouse falling in love with a third party. The eagerness of this one is balanced by the other spouse, who may be very shy of trying again, depending on how ego-bruising the break-up was. Psychological hurts take a long time to heal, and the injured party is likely to approach the idea of remarrying with trepidation. After all, there are no guarantees that the new flame won't result in another searing experience.

All newlyweds, even for the first time, face problems of one sort or another. When they are being married for the second time, the problems that face them tend to be much more complicated.

The second marriage has to contend with certain established behavior patterns or attitudes that may have to be altered. Besides, there are apt to be children of the former marriages on one or both sides, and sometimes they are still dependent or not yet totally out on their own. They do not always take kindly to their parent's new partner, or the partner may not take kindly to his step-children. Comparisons consciously or unconsciously are bound to be made between the former spouse and the replacement, and the new spouse may feel in competition with the old.

Nevertheless, the high rate of remarriage among members of the Middle Generation indicates that a strong faith in the institution of marriage still prevails, along with a great deal of confidence in the future. This is becoming almost a hallmark of the contemporary middle years.

I

Sometimes, overeagerness to recapture the joys of a former happy marriage can lead a widow to an emotional dead end, especially when she is in her middle years. The kind of relationship in which she becomes involved must be examined by her to determine whether it will satisfy her short-term or long-term needs. A glamorous "affair" may have its excitement, but at stake may be the woman's chances to establish a secure, mature relationship with someone more suitable.

This is the problem which the writer of the following letter had to face.

LETTER: *I am nearing forty-four and have been a widow for almost three years. We had no children. In the last year or so, I have managed to adjust to my new life. I have a good job in a large office.*

I have met a man fifteen and a half years younger than I am. He has never been married. I am very fond of him. He says he loves me and wants me very much. I have resisted having an affair with him because I am afraid of how it will end. I know it could not last too long, and in the end I will be rejected because I am the older one.

My best friend tells me I should give in and enjoy it while it lasts. But I am afraid.

ANSWER: No matter how happy and fulfilled a person may be, everyone occasionally needs the reassurance and feeling of approval that come from being sought out and wanted. This need naturally is greater in a person who has experienced a threatening illness or suffered the death of a loved one. It is present even after a divorce which the person herself may have wanted.

Upon the death of a beloved mate, the survivor naturally feels that she has come to the end of her world. She always feels guilty about her gratitude for having been by-passed by death. This makes her feel disloyal to the departed. A re-evaluation of one's performance after a bereavement always points up things that could have been done for the departed to make him happier.

The guilt is universal, but it passes with time. However, when the guilt is excessive or disproportionate, it can keep the person from venturing forth to build a new life for herself. This inhibition may be shown in various ways. She may make herself totally unavailable and then complain that she has no opportunities to meet available men, suitable for marriage. Or else, she may socialize, but when an offer of marriage is made to her, certain faults in the suitor appear suddenly, which she had never noticed before.

Another way is to make herself available sexually only to those completely unavailable for marriage. In this way, by not marrying, she can be loyal to the love of the past, while at the same time gratifying her desires and allowing herself to "play the field," as she had secretly wanted to do before, but never did. Having been married once, and having had an intimate sex life, sex outside of marriage somehow becomes more permissible in this kind of circumstance.

Any woman in her middle forties is bound to feel complimented when a male so much younger wants her. It makes her feel very much younger, too, and she is grateful. The fact that he is almost young enough to be her son seems like a guarantee that this relationship will stem the flow of time, and forever keep her young.

The test of a mature person is the ability to give up passing pleasures for future gains. Such a person is fully aware that the pleasure of today might become the pain of tomorrow. Your friend's advice that you should enjoy it while you can is really rather uncomplimentary, and can only add to feelings of insecurity. It says that it is getting awfully late for you, and you will probably find nothing better.

Actually, to become involved with a person with whom there is no promise of a future together is to waste your time.

When you free yourself from this involvement, you will find opportunities for meeting more mature men, who will want to date you. Your self-esteem will then increase, and so will your chances for remarriage.

II

The reaction patterns and values of one marriage will not, as a matter of course, fit a second marriage. There are bound to be clearly defined differences, especially where the children of one or both previous marriages are concerned. Any children can add much to the life of a childless couple. Nothing so rounds out and fulfills the relationship between a husband and wife as the offspring they produce.

When the survivors of two marriages with such backgrounds as a childless and a child-blessed marriage come together and produce children of their own, it can create problems. One cannot avoid bringing one's past into the new relationship, as this couple discovered.

LETTER: *I have been married for twelve years to a very fine, considerate man. This is my second marriage. My first husband died. I had two children with my first husband, a married son, twenty-eight, and a daughter, twenty-five who doesn't live with us. I have a boy, nine, and a girl, ten, by this marriage. It is also a second marriage for my husband. He was married for twenty-five years. His wife also died. They never had any children.*

Now that he has two lovely children, he just doesn't have any patience with them. He can't stand the way they eat, and he reprimands them all the time. If we eat out in a restaurant, it always winds up in an argument. He claims I don't teach them and that they eat like pigs.

The children are very upset about this. When the boy was only three, he used to chase him away from the table, and I had to feed him in his bedroom.

I know he loves them dearly. What shall I do to straighten out this situation?

ANSWER: While it is a second marriage for both of you, it is your husband's first experience with being a father. Parenthood to you was a natural continuation of a loving experience which began before your present husband entered your life. Also, the two of you were older than the average couple when you began to build a family together.

Routines of living tend to get set over the years, with a concurrent loss of flexibility. This makes adjustment to new situations harder. In his first and childless marriage he was both king and prince, around whom the household revolved. There was no one to disturb the peace or question his wisdom, and no one to compete with him or challenge his ways.

With the coming of your children, he was deposed in one way and pushed aside in another. In the rearing of the children, you were naturally the authority because of your background of long experience. As little children in the home, your young ones naturally were in the foreground of your attention and care.

To counter these assaults on the position to which he had long been accustomed, he chose an area in which he could reassert himself as an authority and become the center of attention. He did so by instigating the fight.

To some people, eating and the manner in which it is done has a much deeper meaning than just the process necessary for sustaining one's energy and health. Things like how much a person puts into his mouth at one time, the way he does it, the movements in mastication and swallowing, the speed with which food is devoured, the slow and careful examination of every morsel before it is put into the mouth, the noises accompanying chewing, may become annoying in themselves.

What is often disturbing to the person sensitive to lack of manners in eating is an unconscious psychological association between eating and early childhood fantasies about sex. Many young ones believe that children are conceived through the mouth, the baby-seed being taken in like food, which then fattens the mother's body and enlarges her belly. Even when they learn later that this is not true, old feelings of revulsion and guilt for having such ideas (and perhaps even wishes in this area) may return. A perfect ritual is then set up to protect against the return of these offensive memories. This is rationalized and incorporated into the person's feelings in the name of good manners, and it becomes a dictum for proper eating.

People will often also repeat in their children's rearing the very methods that brought them unhappiness in their own. A quarrelsome, bickering atmosphere at mealtimes in their own childhood, which they hated as children, may have become transformed in memory, with the years, into an expression of love and concern from the parents. Such retrospective glorification makes possible and often insures the continuation of undesirable patterns into the next generation.

However, you too might re-examine some of your own reactions in the situation when the family gets together at table. Your husband's criticism of some of the children's practices at the table, which may be justified in part, is, however, basically a criticism of you.

The permissiveness with which you handle your children may be too much like that of a grandmother to her grandchildren. Your husband may not like being treated like a grandfather to his own children.

The occasions of family eating should not be used to show the children that you are on their side, protecting them from the onslaughts of their father. Even if you disagree with his demands on them, it is better for them to see their parents standing together, on the same side. You might also go over beforehand some of the niceties their father wants them to observe, and make sure they have learned them.

Mealtimes could then be the times when they show progress and are given approval by their father. The acceptance by them (and by you) of their father's ways will make the children's ways more acceptable to him.

Then peace will replace the battle of the table.

III

Step-children can influence the attitude or approach of the new step-parent toward her family responsibilities. A newcomer entering the family that was grown and well-established by the time she arrived on the scene, experiences built-in competition from the children, no matter how much her husband loves her and wants her to be the mistress of the household. She is also apt to see the familial patterns and relationships through more objective eyes. But her fresh, valid insights cannot always overcome the misconceptions based on long years of misunderstanding of what are proper roles for the family's members.

Such was the case in this family.

LETTER: *I am presently happily married to a widower with two grown children, twenty-five and thirty-one. We get along well enough on the surface.*

My stepson is overattached to his older and unmarried sister. When their mother died, my step-daughter took over her mother's place. She is by nature jealous and possessive. Neither child is very popular with the other sex. They have each got their own apartments and live alone. This happened when we married.

The boy sees his sister constantly and talks of no one else. Now I am afraid outsiders will see how unhealthy it all is. She seems to need his adoration, and is overprotective of him.

My husband distrusts therapy and would not listen to my suggestion that his children need it.

ANSWER: At the beginning of a second marriage it is inevitable that comparisons should be made between the new mate and the old one. Having adjusted to the habits of the former mate, those of the new one may seem different and annoying.

If the children are small, the new mate, on becoming the new parent, can take over and become the loving authority and disciplinarian. But when the children of the former marriage are grown, a screening process takes place before the grown children and the new mate accept each other.

The children, even though they are grown, may see their parent's remarriage as a desertion of them. At times, the parent feels that, in loving another, he has left his children.

A girl who doesn't get married but occupies herself mainly with the care of her family is bound to her father, even though it shows up in devotion to her brother. In taking on all the duties and responsibilities of her mother as the mistress of the household, her old childhood dream of replacing the mother was realized in part.

When the father remarried, she was deposed from this preferred position. She then went through a kind of emotional separation and divorce, in which the new wife became the "other woman" in her father's life.

You may be right that your step-daughter is jealous of you and very possessive of the males in her family. However, the fact that both these grown children moved out and took their own apartments is a good sign. They are evidently beginning to move forward on their own, in the hope of building a life of their own. Perhaps the young man is so laudatory and adoring of his sister because he feels she needs the build-up to compensate for being analyzed and criticized by the newcomer in the family.

Your husband may be not too trustful of therapy because of your recommendation that his children go for it. Therapy is to do for them what he failed to do.

You ought to concentrate on being a good wife to your husband, without competing with his daughter, or trying to show her how a woman should behave in order to get a husband. Whatever they do from here on in, they have to do by themselves. If you accentuate the positives, then perhaps the negatives now seemingly present in their responses to you will become less.

PART III

Middle Generation Parents as Children

✄ 13. MIDDLE GENERATION PARENTS

The contemporary Middle Generation is generally better educated and better informed than its predecessors, and has new insights into the nature of parent-child relationships, both as children to their own aging parents, and as parents to their own children.

Contemporary emphasis on geriatrics and the sociology of old age has illuminated what their parents are facing. Perhaps they are more sympathetic because they have a fairly good forecast of what they, themselves, will have to face eventually.

Nevertheless, sons and daughters, no matter what their age or how established their own families are, are forever seen as children by their parents. The way they were treated in childhood tends to be carried over by their parents into their adult lives. Reciprocally, it governs their conduct toward their aging parents to a great degree.

Today's Middle Generation still has to deal with many of the same problems their predecessors did—the care and support of aging parents who can no longer manage for themselves; the role of old-age homes; living under the same roof with aging parents and utilizing, controlling, or mitigating their influence on the young children; parental remarriages after death of a mate; debility, disability and senility, as well as emotional deterioration, in the older generation; and the like.

How is the present Middle Generation coping with these problems?

Generally speaking, quite well, though some do better than others, and some problems are inherently more difficult than others. However, with more and more Middle Generation parents around, as the decades roll on, we shall have to learn to cope more and more effectively.

I

Emotionally dependent parents can be as burdensome in their own way as young children, sometimes even more so. The Middle Generation woman who wrote the following letter faces just such a situation.

LETTER: *I am married over twenty years, have two boys, thirteen and eighteen, and a wonderful husband. My father died over four years ago. Since then, it seems that my mother's main object is to make my life miserable. We are a quiet family. My life revolves around my home and we have a few groups of friends.*

When my mother comes to visit, about twice a week, I must sit and talk with her. If I am busy with something, she gets very angry. She was always a little domineering and recently has become more so.

I have reached the time in my marriage to which every woman looks forward. The children are grown and I am free to come and go with my husband, whenever or wherever I want. Usually, I ask my mother along, but there are times when I want to go out alone with him. Then she makes a fuss, and acts like a spoiled child. She sulks for a few days and doesn't come to visit to punish me.

She had a world of friends and belonged to different organizations, but she dropped all that except for some friends in her building. I used to be very close to her. But she has changed so much that I don't feel that closeness any more.

When I am with her, I am always under tension. I was getting myself very sick over this, until I decided that this is how she is and that I have to take it. But I am losing patience with her.

ANSWER: The fact that your boys have grown up has given you a sense of freedom which you evidently felt their coming had taken from you. Now, you can once again recapture with your husband the romance and glamour of the courting period and the honeymoon years.

Your return to the side of your husband, with renewed and deeper companionship than you ever had before, is also good for your boys. They derive a freedom from your freedom, and will not be exposed to a mother who justifies her own existence by her children's dependence on her.

You, yourself, however, have been overly dependent on your mother for too long. Perhaps her close presence when you needed her during the early years was of great comfort and help to you. When the responsibilities of motherhood weighed you down, you could depend not only on her help, but also on her approval of you as a wife and mother. This evidently meant a great deal to you.

After your father died, when her demands upon you really became great, you still did not mind too much. You were tied down anyhow by your sons, who, at nine and fourteen, still needed your attention. So having another person around was not too great a burden. Besides it also helped you in your mourning when you were good to your mother in her grief.

Now however, the roles of parent and child are being reversed, and you find it annoying and unacceptable. When you are free of your own children, you do not want to take on a mother who is acting like a spoiled child, and whose dependency on you suddenly begins to emerge in full bloom. It makes you feel like a deserter, abandoning a helpless person. However, there are other possible solutions.

You cannot free yourself from your mother's domination, while at the same time informing her fully about what you do, where you go and with whom you spend your time. This invites her comments and interference, as if you did not want to give up the role of a little girl asking mommy's approval and permission. Telling her all makes her feel excluded whenever you want to be alone.

Filling up the time she is at your house with duties or chores that could be done at other times is a way of putting her down and saying that you have more important things to do than to sit and chit-chat with her. It would certainly be more polite and gracious to get your little chores out of the way beforehand, and be free to spend time with her when she comes to visit.

You must have freedom to go out with your husband when you wish to do so. Once she perceives that she can no longer tag along with you for her social life, she will return to her former associations or make new ones. It will be much better for her when she resumes her contacts.

She is evidently a capable woman. Once she has recaptured her independence, she will be grateful to you, rather than resentful, for she will then be free of her children, just as you are, and will continue to enjoy living.

II

The keystone of any family is the relationship between the mother and father.

However, the true nature of that relationship may not really be grasped by children until they have matured. It is then that they can begin to understand the family structure and the roles they played within it. They can then perhaps appreciate the complexity of their emotional involvements, as the person who wrote this letter reveals.

LETTER: *This summer, my mother age sixty-seven, died and in November, my father, seventy-four died. My problem is that I cannot mourn for my mother.*

I always loved my mother and considered her an angel. Actually, all of us, my two sisters and three brothers, felt the same way. Our childhood was a series of battles between my father and my mother, fanned to white heat by my oldest sister. My mother was always the martyr, my father always the villain. Everything wrong he did was magnified, and the good things he did—like providing for us well, even during the Depression—were minimized and criticized. We grew up hating my father and now we all find ourselves mourning and weeping more for him than for mother.

After I was married, sixteen years ago, I left my home town and was able to become more objective. Now I have concluded that my father was a victim.

Almost until the day she died, my mother complained about my father behind his back and he loved her so much. She minimized that, too, and said he was a liar. After she died, my father who was always aggressive, strong-willed, and in good health, fell apart. He mourned excessively, and said that he had lost his best friend. He was found dead three months later with a note saying that he couldn't live without my mother.

I try very hard to understand my mother's actions. I need help to get rid of the bitter resentment I feel toward my mother, whom I used to love so much.

ANSWER: In the reaction to a death, the components of love and hate that were consciously or unconsciously felt for the departed are now re-enacted emotionally. There is a strong resemblance in these reactions to the feelings of the adolescent who is growing up and away from the parents.

Love for the parents balances against resentment for needing them, and pulls children in opposite directions emotionally. They feel disloyal for wanting to leave the parents, while demanding so much from them and being so dependent on them.

When the youngsters dream of going off with someone else and leaving their parents behind, feelings of fear or guilt or both, arise and the youngsters often convert these into hostility for the parents. They blame them for not creating an atmosphere of ease and smooth transition, without problems. Gradually, as successful achievement is scored up by the youngsters, their attitudes and behavior change and they begin to appreciate their parents again.

The experience which is distressing you now is to find yourselves loving the parent you hated and hating the parent you loved. However, the anger for the mother, which is now finding expression, was always felt, but was suppressed for a number of reasons. One was that you probably feared to show it against the person who obviously dominated the household. Besides, seeing the man of the house, your father, intimidated, took away any courage you may have had to speak up and rebel against her punishing authority.

You didn't like her for assuming the male's prerogatives, and you didn't like your father for abdicating his. Rivalry between mother and daughter for the father's attention is often incited to white heat by either or both of the parents. It is a parental way of courting, that leads to lovemaking when the lights are off and they are alone.

Your oldest sister fought for all the girls in the family. The boys, who are naturally competitive and rivalrous with the father, didn't mind seeing him vanquished by the females. Thus, they could have the mother, whom they wanted for themselves. When your mother called your father a liar about his declarations of love for her, she may have implied that he loved his daughters too much and her not enough.

Aggressive though your father was in some ways, he loved the treatment he got from your mother. Since he was not basically a fighter, her assaults brought out the aggressiveness in him and made him feel more manly. In counteraction, and self-protection, these attacks served to mobilize all his forces and made him feel the total and integrated man he wanted to be. She befriended him by attacking him. When this catalytic force which synthesized him was removed, he went to pieces. The way in which he chose to die showed his great need for her. She, in dying, was still the aggressor and was responsible for his death.

The children feel it is a condemnation of them when a parent commits suicide. Had they been closer and more loving to him, they feel, he would not have felt so alone and deserted when his wife died, and might have stayed alive. They blame their mother for standing between them and him and building up such a hateful image that they could not be loving to him when he was alive.

Now you feel that in loving your mother too much you did not love your father enough. But it will not help preserve your father's memory to hate your mother in retrospect. You must recognize that for them, theirs was a good marriage, because it fulfilled their basic needs. They bore six children who have grown up and established marriages and loves of their own. These facts in reality are the measuring rod by which their relationship should be judged.

The objectivity you talk of is achieved now only partially. When you have feelings of gratitude and warmth in remembering both of your parents in spite of seeing their weaknesses, you will not have to mourn for one in order to feel love for the other.

III

Older people remarry to an increasing extent because, to an increasing extent, they stay younger longer, both sexually and emotionally. Grown children sometimes react very strongly toward an aging parent's remarriage, especially if it comes very soon after the death of the other partner. When the new wife is much younger, the angers and resentments are multiplied. In fact, as is the case with the "child" who wrote this letter, such an event can bring into the open surprising animosities and emotional distortions.

LETTER: *My parents lived together for thirty-seven years, not too happily. Suddenly, Mother died, leaving Dad, sixty and sick, plus four married children and ten grandchildren. I, the eldest of the children, was also closest to my mother.*

My parents, my husband and I always lived together in the same house. My children's upbringing was supervised by her and any problems they had, sexual or otherwise, they always told her about. Mother took care of everything and managed Father's money wisely, leaving substantial trusts for the children.

Exactly three months after our loss, Dad married a young woman. I don't have to tell you the shock and grief this caused me.

I still cannot forgive him. Let me add that if mother came back to earth, she would fully agree with me that "There's no fool like an old fool!" My brother and sister do not agree with me, and see him and his new wife socially.

ANSWER: Unquestionably, it is rather precipitate when a person remarries only three months after the death of a mate. But sometimes the very people who disapprove of it most are most responsible for its occurrence.

You can be sure that your father participated in whatever financial arrangements your mother made for gifts to the children. Yet he, who made the largesse possible, is bypassed and denied approval and recognition, and worse yet, even the thanks due him.

Money may have been used in your family as the medium for getting obedience, and for rewarding such obedience when it was forthcoming. It may have also been used as a means of retaining authority over the family, even when the children had grown up and gone off to build families of their own.

Your father's money rather than your mother's memory seems to be the main reason for the great hostility toward the remarriage. Much of this must have been felt by your father. Being treated like an old, sick man whose life was waning fast might have made him feel that he was being disposed of prematurely. Frightened by this patronizing treatment, he escaped into a liaison with youth. Here was a reality which could reassure him.

He may also have been afraid that you, the oldest daughter, who were so close to your mother, might take over some of the prerogatives and authority which she had assumed.

With your mother, you were always sure that your interests would be protected. With this new wife, you cannot expect this any more.

Your mother will never come back to earth and punish your father for what you feel he has done to you.

You should give up your childish illusion that you can get what you want by becoming a parent to your parent. The attitude of the other children, who are not seduced by the money, is a healthier one. This is shown by their continued relationship with their father and their acceptance of his marriage as the act of a grown-up who knows what he is doing, for his own good. You might well follow their example.

IV

If it is true that the Middle Generation is caught between two generation gaps, it is also true that it is the bridge that spans both. Elderly parents who live with their children and their children's children, frequently illustrate this. There is a compelling need for their Middle Generation children to take on such a bridging role. In the situation presented in the following letter, two extremes of age pose a common problem for those caught in the middle.

LETTER: *Last year, my mother, who is eighty, came to live with us. She had been living in her own apartment with various companions whom she antagonized until they left. She didn't get along with her neighbors.*

I am her only living child. I have two married daughters, twenty-nine and twenty-five, and one, thirteen. We are a close, loving family, and have a good relationship with our in-laws.

My mother constantly picks on and criticizes my thirteen-year-old. When I ask her to leave the child's rearing to us, she gets insulted, accuses us of forcing her to give up her home, and says it is a curse to live so long.

I love my mother and want to make her remaining years happy. I've asked my young one to be patient with Grandma. But this only brings on tears and more resentment. Mother also can't take the two great-grandchildren (three and four), who tend to be a bit rambunctious. She insists that they are spoiled and chides me for loving up these babies.

Fortunately, my husband takes no sides and stays out of it. How can I make this a loving home again?

ANSWER: Self-centeredness under seven and over seventy are appropriate and par for the course, however hard it may be for families to take. In demanding attention and control, they are really asking for protection and care.

The little one's need to dominate and make everyone do his bidding is caused by weakness and helplessness. When the adults give in, the little one feels powerful and controlling, and the inner insecurities disappear for a time.

The controlling and domineering behavior which the aged sometimes manifest stems to a large degree from the same reason. In addition, having once been parents in full control of the family, they feel demoted and dispossessed not to have this power any more. What is even worse, growing older means losing power over themselves, as well as over others. They want, therefore, to be the center of everyone's attention and to be listened to when they hold forth as authorities on every subject.

From this need, there may sometimes stem a rivalry

and competitiveness with the younger children in the family, even more than with the adults. For, while wanting to be mothered, they still want to be the complete mother-authority, listened to and obeyed implicitly.

At this time in your youngest daughter's life, she has enough inner conflicts and fears about herself, her identity and her future, without becoming further confused and conflicted by being picked on and criticized constantly by her grandmother.

To ask that a thirteen-year-old be patient and understanding of the unacceptable behavior of an older adult is rather unrealistic.

Your husband, in agreeing to have your mother come and live with you, has shown great tolerance and understanding. However, greater participation on his part, where he takes over as head of the household, is what is needed. Your mother feels qualified and authorized to tell her daughter or granddaughter off, but would listen with respect when your husband intervenes and protects his child.

Also, since your mother can afford it, she could use some of the money that formerly went for living expenses and companions to pay for extra help around your house or for a part-time companion to take her out at certain times of the day or night. This would relieve you of the additional household burdens and, even more, would give you extra time to spend with your daughter, who needs to see you as a loving mother more than as a devoted and dedicated daughter to her parent.

V

Belief in immortality is part of the creed of many religions. It springs, no doubt, out of the difficulty most people have in facing the concept of death, especially their own death. It is also a projection of the hope to be reunited with dear departed ones in an after-life in which all is free of tension and turmoil and blissful eternally.

Very often the departed one is thought of as being fully informed about all earthly activities of the survivors, and re-acting to them with pleasure, pain, anger, sadness, dis-appointment, and other emotions. When the survivor is a spouse with whom the departed has lived a number of years, the person, or the children of the marriage, are generally expected to live in such a way as not to shame or displease him, and the obligation is often taken to be even stronger than if the departed were still alive.

This becomes poignantly clear when the survivor plans remarriage, and more so in the case of a widower than a widow. The children often feel that the father's remarriage shows disloyalty to their departed mother. If it comes too soon after the death, they may have a real sense of outrage.

In the letter that follows, a son, while professing a wish for his father's happiness, sets up his departed mother's intra-familial hostilities as the criterion his father ought to use in choosing a new mate.

LETTER: *My dad is sixty-eight years young, in good health, and enjoys life. My mother passed away a year and a half ago. They were happily married for forty years.*

He has always enjoyed his family. He has all our re-spect. He is semi-retired, and is financially independent.

He just returned from Florida after a three-month stay and has spoken to me very openly about the women he met there. He wanted to know what my feelings would be if he should remarry. I told him I would go along with what-ever is best for him.

My dad's younger brother died three years ago. His

widow, my aunt, is seven years younger than my dad. She is a good woman and might make a good home for him. After talking about the other women, my father started talking about this aunt.

What bothers me is that she and my mother never got along. If my dad should marry her, I would feel he was betraying my mother.

Am I wrong in siding with the way my mother felt toward my aunt?

How can I help my dad see the direction in which he should go?

ANSWER: A loving child ordinarily wants what is best for his parents, just as they wanted what was best for him.

When one of the parents departs, there is great concern for the one who is now left alone. In the beginning, the grown children may include him in their family activities and keep in constant touch with him. They let him know that they are always available, should he need any help. Being so loving and attentive to the one who has suffered most helps them to express their own grief.

But in time, the child begins to be concerned about how long this dependency on him will last. He is naturally eager to resume his own life, and wishes his father would begin to build a new life for himself.

When the parent has gotten over the period of mourning and is preparing himself to venture into the stream of life again, he experiences some feelings akin to those of adolescents. He wonders if he will be liked and accepted when he starts to socialize again. If his children show any objection or hesitancy about this, he may read into it the message that he is too old to do so, which makes him feel older than his years.

The remarriage of a father is often seen more as disloyalty to the grown children than to the departed mate. Interestingly, it is easier when they have to give up a widowed mother to a new mate, than a widowed father. They reason that a man doesn't really need to get married again. They don't mind if the father "plays the field" and has one date after another. This is a way of enjoying life, while staying close to home base. Then they don't have to share his love or any material benefits that might come to them later, with a stranger. When a widowed mother finds a new mate, it takes responsibility for her care and entertainment off their shoulders, and they are usually delighted for her, as well as for themselves.

In telling you about the women he has met, your father is letting you know that he is ready to enter into a new marriage relationship. You may see the normal disagreements that took place between your mother and aunt as fights that hurt your mother. You may now speculate about whether your father sided enough with your mother, or tended to be too understanding of his sister-in-law. Now, this raises the suspicion that he found her attractive and likeable, even then.

That your father wants to remarry is a great testimonial to the happy life your parents had together. For him to make the right choice, he must do it on his own, and not use his children as marriage counselors. He should marry the woman who is attractive to him mentally, emotionally and physically.

When he makes a choice on this basis, it will be a good one for him. Then he will be happy and fulfilled for the remaining years of his life.

14. MIDDLE GENERATION SIBLINGS

The term sibling rivalry has a familiar ring to all who are psychologically aware, for it is present in every family, along with love and affection. All parents must face and handle it, if they have more than one child.

Strangely enough, it continues to manifest itself among mature siblings belonging to the Middle Generation. However, the ways in which they express it match the circumstances of their older years. They have long since resolved and laid to rest the old causes of inter-sibling friction, like those over household chores, parental favoritism, weekly allowances, permission to date, and so on. The new sibling rivalries are over the care of aged parents, family finances, differences over the upbringing of children, relations with in-laws and other relatives, and other such matters.

Siblings who were bitterest rivals in childhood, often become close and affectionate in later years. Those who got along so well when they were young, sometimes become indifferent or even hostile to each other as they grow older.

I

Usually, the relations that develop between siblings depend on the kind of relationship each one has with the parents, which is, after all, the basic source of any feelings which grow out of any family.

These three sisters are still acting out the sibling rivalry of their early family life, even though they are now established, with families of their own.

LETTER: *We are three sisters who have supported our aging father. For the last ten years, two of us have carried the entire load, while the third, who has considerably less than we do, has been excused from contributing.*

Now, this one is planning a vacation trip. My oldest sister says that from now on she must contribute, or else she will stop. This argument threatens to break up our family.

I am willing to go on as before, but my oldest sister is adamant.

ANSWER: A great religious sage once said, "To give in health is gold; to give in sickness is silver; to give in death is brass."

Too many people wait for a crisis or a great need before they give. Others use giving as a means to control and dominate, or to show how good they are. Giving for the wrong reasons wrongs the receiver as well as the donor, and nobody benefits.

This pattern probably started back when you were all children in your parents' household. The older sister may have felt that the younger one, "the baby," got too much attention and too many undeserved gifts. She, the oldest one, by contrast, had too many duties and responsibilities, and was deprived of her entitlement.

Now she sees her opportunity to retaliate. Because she, the one who had been given so much less, ended up by having so much more, the impulse was held in abeyance these many years, and she had a great feeling of superiority. Playing "Lady Bountiful" to the sister who had once been the pampered one took the edge off her hostility.

The younger sister had so little and had to work so hard for the bare necessities of life, that the older one saw no threat in her, and was quite willing to let her enjoy what she had. But, the moment she began to spread her wings a bit, the long-hidden jealousies flared out into the open.

The real target of the anger now emerging, though totally unconscious, may be your father. For his complicity in the early days in pampering the youngest sister, the oldest one can now punish him. She could not do this when she was young, but now she could deprive him of support, as she felt she was deprived of love by him.

The person who would be hurt the most if this plan should go through is your father. It would not only be from getting less of the money he needs for his support, but also from sensing the hostility felt against his other daughter and against himself.

The support of your father should not be endangered by such internecine conflicts and you should not be intimidated by the oldest sister's threat.

Feeling a bit less strained financially, the younger sister would probably now be willing to contribute toward the support of her father. If this were suggested to her in a way which does not humiliate her or make her feel she has been derelict in the past, she might participate graciously and happily, even though she could not give as much as her sisters.

She may have been holding back in offering to help only because, not having done as well financially as her sisters, she feels inferior. She may think it is demeaning to contribute a smaller share than the others. But if she is made to feel that in giving according to her circumstances she is really doing enough, she may take a different and more appropriate stand.

After all, she works to support her family. By not having become a burden to her sisters, she feels that she has freed them of an obligation which they might otherwise have had to assume. She may figure that, in this way, she is making a kind of contribution, even though a negative one. She may well feel too, that she deserves the contemplated vacation. It is the first time she is allowing herself such a pleasure.

The oldest sister may feel, however, that having been excused for so long a time from carrying her elementary responsibility to her father, assuming it now that she is able to, should be given first priority, regardless of how well-deserved her vacation may seem to be. When the youngest sister suddenly reveals a private cache, which she has been squirreling away all the time, the oldest one may feel betrayed and angry.

Once the younger sister begins to contribute something to the support of her father, she will have a higher opinion of herself. Then, whatever she gives to herself, be it vacations or anything else, will not have guilt associated with it.

However, the way in which this wrong is righted is important. The person who must be given first and foremost consideration is your father. The oldest sister must not bludgeon the youngest one into giving, or use it as a reason to give less herself. The gift and the giving could be adulterated by hostility and rivalry. Your father must not get the feeling that the family is falling apart because of his need for help in his old age.

If your younger sister can be given the feeling that in making a contribution to her father's support, she is now a full-fledged and equal member of the family, you will all be better off. This would be a constructive, rather than a punitive step to take.

II

The first-born in any family usually carries a special burden because of that fact. This is particularly true if the oldest is a female and the death of the mother forces her to become a surrogate-parent to the younger siblings. This puts them in a Middle Generation position with the oldest sibling, though she is really of the same generation as they are. As one sister explains in the following letter, this skewed relationship can bring on its own peculiar problems. The younger ones are confused as to whether the older one is a sister or a mother. The older one has a mother's responsibility, without her authority and without the freedom from sibling rivalry which a mother's position in the family bestows. The love-dividends which accrue in a mother-child relationship are also absent.

LETTER: *I am forty-eight, and the youngest of five. I am married to a wonderful man and have two grown children. My problem is my older sister, fifteen years my senior.*

She is always bringing up the fact that she took over when I was born and raised me. Our mother died first, many years ago, and our father later. The subject of all the sacrifices she has made for me keeps cropping up in front of other members of the family. If I express an opinion which she doesn't agree with, an argument erupts, but I avoid discussions with her that might excite her too much.

*She and her husband are not in the best of health.
They have no children.*

The whole thing is very distressing to me.

ANSWER: In asking payment for ancient gifts of love and consideration, your sister shows how poor she feels emotionally. Some people use giving as a means of keeping others dependent on them. They apparently need this desperately to bolster their self-esteem. Only by giving to others can they justify giving to themselves.

At first, taking over care of the family after the death of a mother makes the older child feel very important. All of the rivalries engendered when a new sibling comes into the family are now channeled into helpful instead of aggressive actions.

Besides, being a substitute mother gratifies the unconscious desire, left over from childhood, to be the first woman in the father's life. However, since doing for others is so noble, playing the mother-role does not engender guilt or shame.

Your sister's reaction is undoubtedly aggravated by the universal feeling all childless couples have, that they are deprived of the best things in life. In compensation, such couples often treat their nieces and nephews in a very loving and giving way. But when the youngsters grow to maturity and begin to lead lives of their own, the childless couple feels deprived and empty all over again.

Your older sister feels twice deserted, because first her parents died and left her, and now the children she reared for them are deserting her. Not being well, her need for attention and concern is great. She would like to maintain the role of mother-figure in the family because only in that way could she remain the center of attention.

At your age and with grown children it is, of course,

difficult to accept being treated like a child. This kind of treatment, meted out in front of others, can be quite a humiliating and annoying experience. However, like all life-long patterns, it is not easy to break.

The most effective way to start might be telling your sister, in a kindly way, how distressing you find it. If she were made more aware of this pattern, it might help her to control it. You might also point out to her that by denigrating others, one really cuts oneself down. Even people who love her may be impelled to stay away, to avoid such treatment.

If you treat her with respect and listen to her tales of woe, even though they may get boring sometimes, it may provide the emotional medication she needs, which may, in time, become less necessary.

Including her, when possible, in your family gatherings, might also help. This would be especially fruitful if her nieces and nephews, whose separation from her is most painful to her, would arrange to invite her to their homes on occasion. This would be more satisfying than visiting her home, even though poor health might sometimes prevent her from accepting their invitations. The main thing is to reduce her feeling of isolation and rejection, which will automatically reduce her need to retaliate.

III

Sometimes, relations between Middle Generation siblings become strained when the years bring with them a widening difference in their social and economic status. It is normal for changes to take place in their attitudes and feelings toward each other.

If they do not face the facts squarely and recognize the

emotional tug which they exert, they will not be able to make the necessary adjustments. The positives which have been built up in their relationship may then be lost.

This letter points up the relevant questions. Who is really straining the relationship and how can what is good and valuable in it be restored?

LETTER: *We are two sisters in our mid-thirties, and happily married. As children, we had an intense rivalry. Our parents gave us everything they could.*

My sister lives in another state. Her husband, a college graduate, makes over $20,000 a year.

My husband is not a college graduate. Our combined income is less than half theirs. We live comfortably but modestly. I, the younger one, married long before my sister did.

My sister and her husband are very generous—embarrassingly so, since we cannot reciprocate in kind. We have the feeling that they look down on us.

If my brother-in-law continues to practice the "put-down," my husband will be increasingly less willing to spend time with him. Recently, they haven't answered our letters. Now I learn that they are coming home for a visit, and don't plan to spend time with us.

Many of my friends tell me that they have similar experiences to mine. When their brothers or sisters have outstripped them socially and economically, they have been unable to remain on good terms.

What should I do? I don't want to hurt my husband or my sister.

ANSWER: Some parents handle sibling rivalry by treating all their children equally. Then they cannot be accused of favoring one over the other. But this deprives them all of the feeling that they are special to their parents, or that they are loved and appreciated for themselves. This does not really help to overcome sibling rivalry. Although it may be suppressed in childhood, in the adult years, the jealousy crops up and may be directed toward the spouse or the children of the sibling.

You see in your sister's generosity a way of denigrating you. If she were less giving you would probably call her stingy and selfish.

It is easier to hold your brother-in-law's affluence responsible for the break in the relationship with you, than to face up to what may really have caused it. You have evidently discussed your sister's and her husband's treatment of you with your friends and family. People who listen to this kind of talk are prone to pass it on ultimately to the person who is being discussed. Your sister may feel that you talk too much to others about private family matters. Not answering your letters may be her way of rebuking you for this.

That outsiders, too, have this problem, may make you feel that you are not alone. But, in the end, revealing your problem makes you feel worse about yourself. It then drives you to find a spurious kind of vindication for your attitude.

The best approach would be if you could talk directly to your sister to clear the air before she comes here for her visit. Then you could write in advance of their visit, inviting them out as your guests for an evening on the town.

Perhaps when you and your husband play the role of the gracious hosts, you will not feel belittled by your sister's generosity.

IV

When siblings find it difficult to express anger and resentment toward each other, sisters-in-law and brothers-in-law often become substitute targets. Their association through marriage sets them up to receive the blows which love or fear deflects from the sibling.

Two sisters-in-law often act toward each other as though they were sisters. However, sometimes their relationship is hampered by the kind of feelings that existed in the past between the husband and his sister. Their hidden hostility becomes a barrier that the spouse finds hard to break down.

Such a situation, triggered by a tragedy, came between the people involved in this case.

LETTER: *Several months ago, my sister-in-law's nephew, twenty-four, a brilliant young man, died. She took it very hard. While he was ill, I called every day. Afterward, I still called.*

Three months later, I asked her over to my house. She refused, saying it was because I did not show any sympathy or come to see her. I hung up.

I asked my brother to come to see me, as I didn't want any arguments between us. He came and said I was wrong. I tried to explain, but he walked out. He said the only way things could be straightened out is if I would come to his house and speak to his wife.

He said also that he would never forgive or forget what I did. This hurt me greatly. My husband says not to go, as I did nothing wrong.

We have two wonderful children, both college students. She has a daughter, eighteen, not too good a student.

They lost their first-born, a boy, at birth. Should I visit them against my husband's wishes?

ANSWER: Closeness between grown and married siblings does not always stem from loving regard for each other. Sometimes it is out of competitiveness and rivalry which has never come anywhere near solution. This rivalry may then be transferred onto in-laws, against whom they feel free to carry on the fight which they cannot bring themselves to pursue against their sibling.

Your sister-in-law feels, with some justification, that life has been hard on her in many ways. Having the attention of someone like you, to whom life has been so good, makes her feel that she has not been rejected altogether. Your sister-in-law no doubt saw in her nephew the son she never had. He evidently had all the assets that any parent would want in a child. Her daughter is probably a disappointment to her in that she is not as gifted and outstanding as the other nieces and nephews.

At her time of great and unbearable distress, you telephoned, but never came. The calls were seen as a way of keeping posted on what was happening, and not as a sign of genuine loving concern on your part.

You may not have wanted to become too involved because you were not too close to the nephew or his family. But, on a deeper level, you may have resented that your brother and his wife paid more attention to the nieces and nephews on her side of the family than to your children. This may well have been your real reason for staying away, though you may not have realized it.

Calling your brother to come to see you in order to straighten things out was undoubtedly resented by your sister-in-law. It said to her that you wanted to keep your relationship with your brother going, but didn't care about her.

The wish to retaliate in a situation like this arises only when a person feels guilty for having caused the dissension. To admit that perhaps one did not do the right thing is a sign of maturity and strength.

Since you are so happy and fulfilled in your own family life, you can afford to be generous with your sister-in-law. You should extend your hand for a reconciliation. Once peace has been reestablished, whatever your brother and his wife may have said in moments of anger and hurt will be put in its proper place.

⚜ 15. BETWIXT AND BETWEEN

Children are natural and welcome consequences of marriage, fulfilling the parents' need for a proof of their mutual love, and assuring the continuity of the family and the perpetuation of the species. They restore to grandparents a sense of renewed parenthood, without any of its pressures or responsibilities.

Grandparents may bring complications into the lives of the adults around them, especially members of the Middle Generation, who find themselves caught between the older generation, their own parents, and the younger generation, their children.

Grandparents are in the middle with respect to their grandchildren. They sometimes find themselves accused of becoming too involved, or of not being involved enough. The grandchildren treat them as another and preferred set of parents, or ignore them altogether. The parents then attack the grandparents for taking over too completely with the grandchildren, or else are hurt by a seeming lack of regard for them. Some grandparents resent the grandchildren for suddenly making them feel their age.

These circumstances can cause misunderstanding, friction and a breakdown in communications.

Parents caught between the two generations may feel forced to treat their own parents as competing siblings of their children. They may find themselves renewing their own adolescent rebelliousness by condoning their children's conduct toward the grandparents.

The parents may find it difficult to assert their own authority in their own home if grandparents live with them. The problem of a parent's advancing age and progressive senility can generate tensions when three generations share the same home.

In spite of these problems, the fact remains that grandchildren actually help to bind a family more closely together. Many a conflict between parents and children that has smoldered through the years is dampened or even extinguished when the children produce offspring of their own. Most grandparents see in their children's children a continuation both of themselves and of their children, a guarantee of immortality of a special kind, which they can enjoy while still alive.

Parents of the grandchildren see in the relationship that develops with their own parents a reflection of the happiest part of their own childhood.

Many would like to return to the safe, secure years of childhood, which were free of all burdens and responsibilities. Experiencing once again the joys of young parenthood, even if vicariously, helps to negate and deny the advancing years. It is frustrating for a grandparent to see it so close at hand, and be a passive spectator, rather than an active participant.

I

What might be called a classic Middle Generation symptom-complex occurs when an aging parent is taken into a child's home. Three generations whose age may span as much as six decades try to get along together under one roof. The inevitable differences in habits and attitudes make it a kind of tight-rope walking exercise for the Middle Generation. There is an inherent sadness in growing old, which, added to the bitterness of dependency upon children, however loving and considerate they may be, makes it all very hard to swallow, for some.

This is highlighted in the poignant example below.

LETTER: *I am married for twenty years to a most kind and consider ate man. We have two lovely children, a son, seventeen, to be a college sophomore, and a teenage daughter. My mother, seventy, has lived with us for sixteen years. I was ten and my sister twelve when my father died. We never wanted for anything, educationally or otherwise.*

My mother doesn't get along with my children. She is constantly criticizing their every move and bickering with them. She has her way or sulks in her room until I appease her. She always dominated me and now, at forty-one, when I act on my own she is deeply hurt.

My children are annoyed because she is always correcting them. I try to keep peace, but find myself siding with them. She doesn't get along with my sister or her husband, so she can't live with them. After my father died, my mother remarried twice and was divorced twice. My husband and I and our children get along very well.

Two years ago, my mother took a long trip. We had the most peaceful, harmonious and loving time in years.

ANSWER: Your dilemma is that along with your natural gratitude and affection, you also feel hostility for your mother's persistent domination, and shame over her two recent marital misadventures. Despite these failures, she operates as the fount and oracle on all subjects and relationships, and wants to be regarded as the final judge.

As people grow older they fear the wavering and diminution of their physical and psychological powers. To compensate for the fear of becoming helpless they try to show strength.

They impose their will and rush to offer advice and opinions before being asked. To have their guidance rejected is to be discarded as worn out and useless.

Your children would take their grandmother's correction in better grace if they did not resent so much her domination of you.

The best answer sometimes for such a woman is to live with people her own age, in a Home. There the social and leisure-time activities are planned and expertly supervised, and days are full. She would probably complain bitterly at first about any such plan. But if you could entertain this sounder idea for her future without guilt feelings, you would see its superiority to a continuation of the present arrangement.

If this proposal is unacceptable to you, then you must assume the role of the kindly but firm parent to your own mother. Just as you would never give in to whining, sulking or temper tantrums on the part of your child, you must not submit to this tactic on the part of your mother. There can be no hope of permanent appeasement.

You might also counsel your children to avoid situations that might trap them into a quarrel. They should respect their grandmother, even though they may not (and need not) agree with her.

II

Children need the feeling not only that they are loved, watched over and taken care of, but also that they are being given limits within which they can operate with safety. Consciously or unconsciously, every child wants the parents to be symbols of both love and authority, towers of strength and bowers of tenderness.

Without usurping the position of the parents, grandparents can project the same kind of image in their grandchildren's eyes. In a truly secure and happy family, they should be able to take the place of the parents, occasionally, without arousing conflict or resentment on anyone's part.

Sometimes, however, as in the case that follows, special circumstances require special understanding on the part of all the adults concerned. The authority that the grandparents can safely exercise without stepping on parental prerogatives needs to be defined.

LETTER: *When our son-in-law, an engineer, completed a foreign assignment out of the country, our daughter wrote and asked if they and their children, five and three, could share our home until he finds suitable employment. We agreed, assuring them that they were all welcome. We enjoy having them, and adore our two grandchildren.*

The arrangement is working out satisfactorily, with but one exception. When the little ones fight or misbehave in the presence of their parents, we leave correcting them to their parents. However, when the youngsters are left with us, we try to correct infractions of good manners, lapses in cleanliness, or bodily functions (naturally, on the level of five- and three-year-olds), at the moment that they occur.

Our children resent this keenly, saying children need

no more than two disciplinarians. We as grandparents—even loving ones—should break up physical fights by saying "stop it," and nothing more. We do not believe we are usurping their rights. We cannot make them understand that we are motivated only by love and concern for the children, at a time when the parents are not there to guide them.

ANSWER: In everyone's life there are more than the two authorities of father and mother. Actually, a child's life begins with only one authority, that of the mother. Later, the growing infant perceives that there is someone else in his life, his father, who has authority over him, and even over his mother. It is then that his real adjustment to people and his acceptance of himself begins.

As the child grows older, an older brother or sister, or some older child in the playground may assume a role of authority. Certainly, when he enters school, the teacher, the principal, upperclassmen and monitors all become authorities to a greater or lesser degree, for this period of time. In the home, maids or babysitters with whom the child is left are also authority figures to the child.

In effect, any older person in whose care the child is left, must in some way demonstrate power to supervise and control, or the young child feels unprotected and defenseless against both his own impulses and possible attacks from others. Loving authorities who care enough to direct a child and show him how to behave are really very much needed in every child's life. They help him to feel happier and gain the approval every child wants. The more there is of this type of authority-figure besides the parents, the better for the growing child. What could be better than two grandparents to enlarge this circle of kind and loving authorities.

It is safe to say that if you, the grandparents, permitted the children to behave in a way that their parents would find objectionable, and just sat back and did nothing to stop or correct them, the children would find something very wrong with their grandparents. Not being considered important enough to warrant correction hurts more than punishment or deprivation for an infraction. The child would also begin to question the justice of his parents' punishment of him for similar misdeeds. Moments of anger at them might make him feel that they were more ogres than parents.

Practically and realistically, as long as the children are in your home and are left in your care, you must have the right to stop them in their tracks when their behavior offends and transgresses the limits of what you think is appropriate for children of their age.

Perhaps it is not so much the fear that you have usurped their rights as parents, as the feeling that they gave up some of the prestige of being parents, that bothers your children. They, the grown ones, have asked to come home again to live for a while in the home of their parents. They are grateful to you, but perhaps a little ashamed and disappointed in themselves for not being able to do better on their own. While they are dependent on you, they need to feel they are strong and unquestioned authorities in some field which nobody will question or usurp. They choose as the testing ground in which to be unequivocal and unquestioned bosses, their own little family unit which they have created, even though it is living in the midst of a bigger family unit, the one from which they themselves came.

If the children report on the grandparents, then they are thus punishing their parents for going away and leaving them in the care of others in a strange country. If it is the parents of the children who ask for these reports, then they are doing a disservice, not only to themselves as parents, but also to their children's attitude toward them. They are preventing the formation of a healthy concept of authority.

However, if it is the grandparents who are doing the reporting, although they may be consciously motivated by an honest desire to tell all, they are subtly suggesting that the parents haven't done such a good job.

A good relationship between these children and the second authorities who have entered their lives can make a great contribution to their adjustment. It can lead to cheerful acceptance of the authority of law and order, later in life, and become a gateway to the discipline of learning which lies just ahead.

III

Sometimes a grandchild, particularly in his very young years, has trouble differentiating between a parent and a grandparent. Which of two maternal figures hovering around him all day long is really his mother? After all, they are both loving, comforting, tender and attentive to his needs. What young child fresh out of infancy is equipped to make the distinction on his own? Yet the distinction must be made clear to the child for his own good. In a case like this one, the question is, how to do it?

LETTER: *I have been living with my daughter, her husband, and her two sons from the day they were born. The older is four, and the younger two. Like a grandmother, I gave the four-year-old as much attention as I could. He was born after my daughter was married for nine years.*

Our problem is that the older boy is so attached to me that he is getting a little impossible and out of hand. When I am around he doesn't want any part of his parents. I have to sit with him while he is watching TV, or eating, or even playing outside.

My daughter and son-in-law have tried to reason with him not to bother Grandma, but he just won't listen. I leave the house every day so that he doesn't have me around all the time. When I return, my daughter tells me he asks for his grandma. I try not to encourage his attachment to me. I take care of the two-year-old only when necessary. He doesn't bother me for a thing.

ANSWER: The greater the number of loving relatives in a child's life, the greater is his security. Naturally, next to the parents a child feels closest to his grandparents. They give much love, dole out little punishment, and ask for so little in return.

When a grandparent takes over completely, no matter what the reason, the child is apt to feel that his own parent is shirking her duties and not taking on all the loving responsibility that she should. It is also somewhat confusing to have his mommy's mother around all the time. His mother, the authority figure in his life, is then seen as another child in the family.

Your four-year-old grandson may also be acting out his sibling rivalry through his overattachment to you. He is saying that he has to share his mother with his little brother, but in compensation, he wants his grandmother all to himself. You are his living "security blanket," and he must hold on tight.

It is emotionally confusing to both children to have each of you take on almost complete responsibility for one of them. The work-load in the house should be redistributed so that your daughter takes care of both children while you, as the loving grandmother, help her with the duties around the house. The two children need to learn from what their mother does for them, what a real mother is like, and also what a loving and helpful grandmother can contribute. You cannot be mother to one, while depriving the other of his share in you as a grandmother.

Your older grandson needs to have both of his parents take over and tell him what he can and cannot do. Wanting you so exclusively is only his way of saying that he wants and needs more of his mother. The father should also spend more time with him.

If you were away from home for community service activities, when you told him later about some of the things you did, it would not represent a threat that you are preparing to leave him for good. From this he would learn an important lesson about the happy reality of family life—that after each separation, there is always a happy reunion.

IV

The relationship between a grandparent and a grandchild is not always a ready-made garment that can simply be put on and worn. It depends to a degree on how involved the grandparents become with each individual grandchild. But to an even greater extent, it reflects the relationship they had with their own child, the grandchild's parent.

A grandchild's reaction to a grandparent may be governed by his own sense of security. The parents' reactions toward him and the way he believes the grandparent feels toward him are important factors in determining this.

It would be comforting to guarantee that when such a relationship is having its difficulties, as in the letter below, a little love and understanding on both sides will certainly help heal the rift. However, the relationship is hardly one between equals. The greater contribution of patience, understanding and love must come from the grandparents.

LETTER: *Each of my daughters, ages twenty-eight and twenty-six, has a little girl, three and a half. The children are as different as night and day.*

One child shies away from me. Since she was born she has never given me a kiss or a hug. Although I cannot warm up to her, I try to treat both children equally. She actually runs away if I try to pet her.

My other little grandchild allows me to kiss and hug her. I cannot understand how a little girl will never kiss or hug her grandma or her grandpa.

We have given her little gifts, and have tried to be very affectionate. But she is indifferent. Truth is, I have never heard her mother or father tell her to give Grandma or Grandpa a hug or a kiss.

Do you think she will outgrow this?

ANSWER: There is no such thing as equal treatment of children in the psychological sense. Even when siblings are treated according to their age and sex, there is still a marked difference in the way they are handled by the parents and also in how the parents feel toward them. This does not necessarily mean that the parents love one more and the other less, although it does happen sometimes. But it does mean that the parents feel differently toward and about them.

Grandparents are less involved with their grandchildren than they were with their own children. Therefore, it is easier to treat grandchildren in what they say is a more "equal" way. But actually, because they are removed and do not have any real responsibility for the grandchildren, it is easier for them to have a favorite. This is usually determined not so much by the child as by the relationship of the grandparents with the parents of the little one.

Sometimes the relationship with a daughter is perpetuated in the relationship they have with their granddaughter who re-evokes the feelings they had toward their own daughter when she was little. Feeling guilty for not having given their own child enough, they will try to make up for it by giving too much to the grandchild.

Little ones are very sensitive to the deep feelings of the grown-ups about them. They have built-in barometers which not only measure the current emotional climate, but can forecast the impending ups and downs. A grandmother who is tense because she feels the scrutiny of the young parents and tries to obey their wishes as to how the little one should be treated, may be felt by the child as withdrawn and ungiving. The little one may then respond by rejecting her, as she feels rejected.

The child that is outgoing, warm and affectionate is usually a secure and loved child. But grown-ups, in their anxiety to do the right thing and please the little one, may frighten her into withdrawing. The child reacts to the tension, rather than to the love that exists deep down.

People cannot be commanded to love. Also, going through the motions of kissing and hugging does not teach one to love. The criticism implied in your statement suggests that many things may be wanting in your daughter's relationship with you. The child should not be used as the tool with which to effect the cure.

In all likelihood, you are more relaxed with your outgoing grandchild because you feel more comfortable with her parents. If you could voice to your other daughter some of the things that make you so unhappy, you might be more relaxed when you are in her home.

In the meantime, continue to bring your little gifts of love to this grandchild, but do not expect payment in hugs and kisses. Be patient and give her the chance to make overtures to you. Some little ones feel overwhelmed by an over-affectionate manner. They feel more in control when they can take the first steps toward people. But basically, for a child to warm up to an adult, she must first feel a real inner warmth expressed toward her.

V

Sometimes grandparents have difficulty defining their own roles within the family structure, particularly when they themselves are still young enough to be included in the Middle Generation. This becomes especially difficult when they watch their own children in action, so to speak, with their grandchildren. Then a compulsion to function once again as parents may make itself felt strongly.

On the other hand, what may really be coming to the fore may be a desire to criticize the grandchildren's parents, especially since one of them is, after all, an in-law. In a situation like the one described below, the role the grandparents would like to play in their grandchildren's lives may be a reflection of their own relationship to the son- or daughter-in-law involved.

LETTER: *We are grandparents; I am fifty-five, my wife, fifty-three. Our married son has a lovely daughter, two.*

Our daughter-in-law was an only child of well-to-do parents. In any situation not to her liking my granddaughter withdraws into a corner, places her thumb in her mouth, and won't talk. They tell her they love her dearly. But they do not give her the kind of personal physical love that we gave our two children. (Our married daughter gives it to her child.) She plays in her crib in the dark for hours before she falls asleep. Sometimes, around 4 A.M., she calls "Mommy . . . Daddy." The parents do not hear, or refuse to answer.

We know this because we baby-sat several times. We

try to give her the love she needs, but she still becomes moody when frustrated. My son and daughter-in-law are college graduates. This was a wanted child and they are planning another.

This child has the finest clothing, the best toys and dolls and plenty of space to play in. They own their own home.

We feel that my granddaughter is harboring an inner resentment. She does not cry, but uses this mechanism as a subterfuge.

She is beautiful and bright. Is there anything that we can suggest to the parents without causing friction?

ANSWER: The ways of rebellion and retaliation in childhood are many. There are children who scream and cry to get their resentment out of their system, and others who withdraw from their parents or from the unpleasant situation. Sometimes, by their silent disapproval, these children yell at their parents much more loudly than otherwise.

As life becomes more interesting and stimulating for a child, it also can become more threatening. The little child cannot manipulate the parents' relationship to suit herself. She loves them both, but wants each to love her first and exclusively. She is afraid that if either one were to find out how she feels about the other, she would be abandoned by both. There is no pat or specific way for parents to behave in the situation, and each child has its own way of reacting. As long as the child feels loved, she will, in time, go on to the next phase of development.

Every child will place her thumb in her mouth in times of fear, hurt or hunger. This does not make her a thumbsucker. Long after a child has given it up altogether, she will revert to it when she is going through a turmoil. Certainly at the age of two, a child cannot be called a bedwetter if she still wets her bed. Neither can a child be called a thumbsucker if she still sucks her thumb in times of distress.

At this age too, all children normally become wakeful on occasion in the middle of the night and call for their mommies and daddies, or want to get into their bed. Generally, parents do well to be firm as well as loving and not give in to these demands too often. Of course, in special or unusual situations, as in an illness, a thunderstorm or the like they will naturally give in. However, when this becomes a daily routine, the child gets so much pleasure from the attention given to her that she does not want to give up the infantile behavior. This can hold back and retard the child's psycho-sexual development.

Most parents are willing, at times, to admit that they made mistakes in the rearing of their children, but paradoxically, once they become grandparents, suddenly their way becomes the only right way for their grandchildren. Often this is just a subterfuge for expressing hostile feelings toward the daughter-in-law. If they criticized her as a person, that would make them the typical complaining in-laws. But when the hostile talk concerns the health and welfare of their grandchild, then the criticism can be made freely.

You may feel resentment against your daughter-in-law because she was an only child and was spoiled. You may think that she still wants to be the center of the stage, and doesn't give enough to her own daughter. Since what she has is given to her by your son, you may feel a bit jealous about your daughter's financial position as compared with that of your daughter-in-law.

It is not constructive to raise doubts about whether these parents love their child, or to make them come forth with a protest that they love their child very dearly. Problems of grandparents visited upon parents may have their effects on grandchildren. That these young, knowledgeable people want another child demonstrates their love for the first child and for each other. Any suggestion about how they should handle their child will be seen as a criticism.

For your love to come across to your grandchild, you must show more love to her mother. Little ones are perceptive of hostility and exclusion on the part of the grandparents toward their mother. It threatens their security and makes them frightened.

Your son and his wife may feel that you put too much emphasis on the physical expression of loving feelings. To get their point of view across to you, they may purposely express their affection only verbally when you are around. They must appreciate and respect you, or they would not ask you to baby-sit for their beloved child. You must show the same respect for them. You should not impose your own patterns of behavior on them by requiring that they or their daughter behave the way you want them to.

Act like a loving grandparent and leave the job of rearing your grandchild to her parents.

♯ 16. CONCLUSION

Having looked at today's Middle Generation, it may be fruitful, in conclusion, to look ahead and speculate about the future. In twenty years, the "under thirty" group will be between thirty and fifty years old themselves, and will have married and founded families of their own, as the on-going thrust of life and human relationships demands. They, themselves, will be faced with the rebellions of the next generation of adolescents, and will have their elderly parents, the present Middle Generation, to deal with. They will have become "The Establishment," the Middle Generation of tomorrow.

Will their experiences be any different from those of the Middle Generation of today?

For one thing, we may expect a population of around three hundred million, according to U.S. Census estimates. With so many people, we may expect a corresponding number of problems. Some will be extensions and exaggerations of old problems, and some will be new ones, unique unto the situation that will prevail in the future.

The Middle Generation, as noted, comprises roughly those from twenty-five to fifty-four years old. By 1990, they will grow from seventy to one hundred million people. The fifty-five-and-over group will grow from forty to fifty million, while the younger group, those under twenty-five, will increase from the present ninety-five to over one hundred and twenty-five million. Tomorrow's families will normally include both sets of grandparents, and a great-grandparent or two, making four generations, not three, the standard family pattern, in the next generation.

With the ballot granted to those from eighteen to twenty-one, the new voter group will, by 1990, number 15 million— a sizable bloc in any political arena. They can be expected to influence foreign policy in the direction of reducing the possibility of our getting into future wars, and domestic policy in the direction of remedying any still-existing social, racial, or economic inequalities. However, the natural swing of the generation pendulum will probably make the adolescent rebellion of the 1990s neither as dramatic nor as drastic as that of today. In the 1930s, the younger generation was involved in the labor movement and in radical and anti-fascist causes; in the 1950s, youth was apathetic and passive; in our day, it has become radical and activistic again. Will the pendulum swing back to the conservative side with the youth of the 1990s? If so, they may find their parents far ahead of them in social understanding and as a force for the amelioration of the ills of society.

The Middle Generation of today has won its spurs, and perhaps even an accolade or two, in the battle for social justice, racial equality, and fairer distribution of both the goods and the opportunities of the world. This fact tends to be overlooked in an era of activism and extremism, when gradualism is in bad repute.

In the next generation, tremendous enrichment of the cultural and spiritual lives of the people in all areas and levels of our society should be achieved when the shortened work week adds many hours of leisure to our lives. By automation, computerization, utilization of atomic energy for peacetime purposes, and other devices for the simplification of the mechanics of everyday living, an era of ease and plenty will be possible in the material life. If the idealism of the young will prevail and become a potent driving force when they are older, not only what they are "against" but what they are "for" will be translated into the semblance of a just society. The older generation of tomorrow will support their hands in this work.

The exciting era ahead will be characterized by new concepts, translated into new forms. Cities, for example, may be rebuilt totally, as surface communities of homogeneous, like-interest people, living in the midst of park-cities, surrounded by all the facilities for education, recreation, and creative living. Business and industry will go underground, supplied by subterranean delivery and collection systems, and powered by atomic energy, without pollution. We will take an elevator down to work, instead of going downtown, eliminating the need for roads, cars, and buses, except for intercity transportation, which will be by speedy overhead or underground means, like those available only experimentally now.

With the new home-technology, housekeeping may be as different in the 1990s as the present is from running a home on a farm in the days before rural electrification, refrigeration, "cooking with gas," frozen foods, and supermarkets. There will be fewer women of the next Middle Generation taking care of their own homes, and more of them out at work. Now, the married women in the labor force number twenty-two million, and by 1990, it is expected that there will be forty-five million homes without a mother during the working day.

How will the children of tomorrow be taken care of? The answer will come from the many women who are today successfully pursuing careers, without depriving their children of loving attention and care. It will be with the aid of wider knowledge and more effective techniques of child rearing, day-care centers, specially trained personnel, like in the Israeli Kibbutzim, and other institutions and agencies that will be devised. The mothers will make up in quality and intensity what is lacking in time spent with their children.

While the push of the mothers has been centrifugal—away from the home, that of the fathers will unquestionably be centripetal—back toward the home, in years to come. The absorption of the father in the task of making a living in the competitive milieu of today has often led to his emotional or spiritual absence, even while he was physically present. This left the burdens of discipline, direction and decision-making in many homes up to harassed mothers, themselves frequently suffering from feelings of desertion and neglect. The men of the 1990s will have all the leisure they need to devote themselves once again to the rewarding tasks of being loving mates to their wives and real fathers to their children. The restoration of the loving leadership of the father to the family could reverse the tide of family disintegration which has flooded us with delinquency, addiction, and despair, and once again give children the bedrock of security on which their characters must be built.

The "sexplosion" of the present generation will, no doubt, affect future generations as well. It is likely to settle into a less permissive premarital pattern, with early marriage more the rule, for the young. For the married, a less inhibited and more gratifying love life will prevail, strengthening the bonds of matrimony, decreasing divorce and extramarital affairs. For the oldest generation, there will be a more permissive late-marriage pattern, allowing their love of life to express itself also in a love life. The young will see that the shared responsibilities of marriage are no more demanding than the less formalized living together in the nonmarried state, with which some of them are experimenting today. The Middle Generation may find in sex re-education, perhaps of the Masters and Johnson type, a new form of self-discovery, as well as an extension of the horizons of their mutual relatedness. Older citizens may find in the breakdown of their isolation from the opposite sex, a new kind of rebirth, their tender care for each other and the mutual helpfulness and understanding that they can give each other, and that they so desperately need, supplementing what is left of romantic love in their lives.

With heart disease and cancer conquered, and longevity greatly increased, the concept of retirement, which now hobbles competent members of the older generation, will become broader and more flexible, and no longer an age-determined entity. Society will recognize the wastefulness of discarding competence, experience and wisdom just because it is resident in an older head. It will give retirement a "suspended sentence," utilizing whatever skills and talents are still fresh, as long as the individual can function effectively, full time or part time, in commerce, industry, the arts and sciences, and other areas. The academic world has afforded us an instructive example. The current shortage of college teachers is being met, in part, through the hiring of retired professors. The smaller colleges can afford to pay modest stipends which, supplementing their retirement pension, enable the older professors to remain alive, alert, and useful. The student derives a high order of instruction and inspiration, and the whole college community benefits from the stimulation and prestige which these vital oldsters bring to it. This procedure, extended to other areas of productive work, will be equally rewarding to all parties involved. The aged would no longer be doomed to congregate in minimal-subsistence retirement enclaves, leading a life of vegetative futility. The glowing encomiums about the "Golden Age" will come true when the debilitating "accent on youth" is relinquished in favor of a policy of maximal utilization of needed competencies, no matter in whom they reside, regardless of age.

The system of education that will prevail in the future will be vastly different from anything we now know. The spectacular advances in the collection, storage, and dissemination of information, will make education multifaceted, relevant to the needs of all, and enormously effective. Microfilm, computers, duplicating devices, the vast potential of the communications networks for reaching millions, teaching machines and devices, and techniques now undreamed of, will expand our educational horizons, so that in addition to the skills needed for everyday living, tremendous cultural dividends will be available for all who desire them.

Yet, without basic motivation for living, of a quality to supply valid and inspiring reasons for carrying the burdens of existence, many would continue to escape into the various nihilistic modes of life so popular among the young today. This is where a revitalized form of religion, already foreshadowed today, will come to play an enormous role in the next generation. There is a basic love of ritual in all people, especially in the young. We see this in their communal living patterns, their love-ins, their sing-ins, their particular styles of dress and hair-grooming, their dedication to the same kind of ear-shattering rock music, their protest stereotypes, their anti-Establishment ideology, even their fads of astrology and tarot. Religious ritual may attract them if it is coupled with dogmas and affirmations relevant to the problems of the day. The involvement of religious bodies in the social concerns of our communities, and the ferment among the younger ministers, priests, and rabbis are a good sign. If religion is brought up to date and is made to concern itself with the amelioration of life in this world, rather than with bliss in the world to come, it will flourish and bring the help that is sorely needed. It will give sound answers to the question of the whys and wherefores of existence, and offer counsels of challenge and affirmation, rather than of withdrawal and dogmatic negation.

As the last decade of the twentieth century dawns, there will, no doubt, be many new problems. The philosophers and educational experts say that without problems, there can be no progress, for what triggers the human thinking process is a problem which cries out for solution.

Despite the turmoil and disruption that it has lived through, the present Middle Generation has scored up a respectable record for itself. The next Middle Generation, guided by the experience of its predecessor, may enjoy even greater triumphs in learning, loving and giving, which together spell living.

This is the challenge of the next twenty years for the Middle Generation.

INDEX